THRICE UPON A TIME

For Carol,

Best Wishes,

[signature]

14-6-90

NEW CANADIAN NOVELISTS SERIES

The New Canadian Novelists Series from Quarry Press charts new directions being taken in contemporary Canadian fiction by presenting the first novel of innovative writers.

Other titles in the series include *Mona's Dance* by Ann Diamond and *Ritual Slaughter* by Sharon Drache.

THRICE UPON A TIME

Genni Gunn

Quarry Press

Copyright © Genni Gunn, 1990

All rights reserved.

Special thanks from the author to The Canada Council
Explorations Program; to Bob Harlow, Verbena Donati, and
Barbara Carter for reading and invaluable comments;
to *Trois* and *The Northern Review* in which several poems
previously appeared; and to Simon for intangibles.

The publisher thanks the Ontario Arts Council and
The Canada Council for assistance in publishing this book.

CANADIAN CATALOGUING IN PUBLICATION DATA

Gunn, Genni, 1949-
Thrice upon a time

(New Canadian novelists series)
ISBN 0-919627-81-1

I. Title. II. Series.

PS8563.U572T47 1990   C813'.54   C90-090163-2
PR9199.3.G86T74 1990

Cover art by Wee Láy Láq.
Design and imaging by ECW Type & Art, Oakville, Ontario.
Printed and bound in Canada by Hignell Printing, Winnipeg, Manitoba.

Distributed in Canada by University of Toronto Press, 5201 Dufferin Street,
Downsview, Ontario M3H 5T8 and in the United States of America by
Bookslinger, 502 North Prior Avenue, St. Paul, Minnesota 55104.

Published by *Quarry Press, Inc.*, P.O. Box 1061, Kingston, Ontario K7L 4Y5
and P.O. Box 348, Clayton, New York 13624.

CONTENTS

PREMISE: The Mystery of Gitrhawn

SUBTEXT: The History of Henry and Laura

PREMISE: The Discovery of the Diaries

TEXT: The Diary of Elise

PREMISE: The Case Studies

Coda

PREMISE:
The Mystery of Gitrhawn

THE PRINCE RUPERT SENTINEL, April 13, 1987

> ## Police Seek Your Help
>
> RCMP are seeking the public's help in trying to identify an infant found abandoned in a canoe near the mouth of the Nass River. Prince Rupert fisherman, Gordon Scott, rescued the infant and rushed her to Prince Rupert General Hospital where she lies in satisfactory condition.
>
> Baby G is approximately four weeks old, female and Caucasian. Anyone who has information about the infant's mother is asked to contact Prince Rupert RCMP at (604) 624-0000.

Paul Evans stares at the rain beating hard against his office windows. He hates the rain and he hates Prince Rupert. He might have taken his holidays this month, were it not for the file that lies open on the desk in front of him. They found the baby two weeks ago. Still no clues as to the mother's identity.

He can't believe that no one knows her. A pregnant woman. She must have friends. Paul has checked the hospitals in the area; he has even called on several midwives. Nothing. He slaps the file a couple of times. Women. He'll never understand them. He wonders if they have a network — like spies — secret rules and regulations. Covert. This pregnant woman cannot have been so alone. He shakes his head and buzzes his secretary on the intercom.

"Anybody call?" It's absurd and he knows it. She would have put the call through. He hasn't left his office all morning.

"No, Paul."

He releases the button and leans in his chair. Props his legs on the desktop and stares out the window. Although he faces the harbor, today the thick grey of fog opaques the view. Nature's cataract. Low clouds fill the earth's pockets, smooth out rough edges. He can see the ferry shuttling passengers to Dighby Island, to the airport. One of two escape routes from Prince Rupert, although as often as not, planes are grounded in the fog. The other route is a highway — 900 miles south to Vancouver. Within seconds the ferry disappears into the haze. Paul makes himself imagine a sunny day — few and far between — the luxurious velvet of evergreens on the banks, and the fishing boats bunched together like bumper cars at a carnival. Today, only tips of masts and trolling poles are visible, as if woven against the cloud canvas. Anxiously awaiting the first salmon openings. Paul wishes he could so easily escape his landlock, to be adrift on massive waves.

He sighs, then springs forward in his chair and opens the file. There is the baby's photograph; the doctor's report; the fisherman's account of the find and rescue; a photograph of the canoe (which no one has identified or claimed); the report filed by the officer on duty when the baby was brought in; and last, but most intriguing for Paul, a thick manuscript. It was in the canoe next to the baby, wrapped in a waterproof bag. Handwritten. No author's name.

Paul has spent the weekend reading it, combing it for clues. As far as he can tell, it's a fictional story set over a hundred years ago, in a different part of the province. Perhaps she's a writer, or a researcher, he thinks. The dates and places appear to be accurate. Barkerville. Mid-1860s. He shakes his head again and taps the rubber end of the pencil against the file. He's waiting for a call from the archives in Victoria. He's requested a cross-check on some of the names that appear in the manuscript. Perhaps they're real.

The intercom buzzes and Paul starts in his chair. "Yes?"
"I've got a telex for you. The one you've been expecting."
"Bring it in, what're you waiting for?"

TELEX 01127361
DETECTIVE PAUL EVANS
PRINCE RUPERT RCMP DETACHMENT
MAY 2, 1987

AS PER YOUR REQUEST: LAURA STEWART CHECKS OUT. CHURCH RECORDS AVAILABLE ONLY AFTER THE FIRE OF 1868. BIRTH RECORDED THE FOLLOWING YEAR: CATHERINE STEWART. LAURA STEWART DECEASED TWO MONTHS LATER. PABC FILES LIST CATHERINE STEWART AND JAKE CALDER. CATHERINE STEWART MARRIED PHILIP ANDREWS IN VICTORIA IN 1904. RELOCATED PRINCE RUPERT SEPTEMBER 1908. ONE CHILD, TIMOTHY. CHECK OUT YOUR END. PHILIP ANDREWS ENGINEER FOR GRAND TRUNK RAILWAY. GOOD LUCK.

"Annie, I'm going up to records," Paul tells his secretary. "Take messages." He's got a link. Perhaps he'll be able to take his vacation after all.

Most of the Grand Trunk files he needs are at the Public Archives in Victoria. The woman must be related to Philip Andrews, Paul thinks. And if she was able to find information about her ancestors, he'll find out about her. He's already checked all the Andrews in Prince Rupert with no success. There is a reference to Vancouver in the manuscript, but there are four columns of Andrews in the phonebook. He'll dial each one, if he can't find anything else.

He goes back to his office and calls Annie in.

"Would you be willing to fly down to Victoria with me for a couple of days, Annie? I need some things at the archives and you'd be a big help."

She grins. "What? No indecent proposal?"

"Not this time. Just legitimate work." He smiles.

"I suppose so. When?"

"As soon as you can arrange it. I'll clear it. Before the weekend if possible."

"You got it."

They sit side by side, Paul in the middle, Annie in the window seat. She keeps her head turned, forehead leaned against the glass.

"Nothing to see from this far up," Paul says. "Just clouds."

She turns and looks at him, a disapproving look, he thinks.

"That's all they are," he mutters. "Just clouds."

He reproaches himself. She probably is thinking how insensitive he is. He only said the thing about the clouds because he wants to begin a conversation with her. He'd like to ask her opinion about the case. She's been staring out of that window for the past fifteen minutes.

"Is there something you want to talk to me about?" she asks.

That's what he likes about Annie. He sighs. "Well. The case, of course. You'll have to know what to look for once we get there."

"I've read the file," she says.

"The manuscript?"

"No."

Paul reaches for his briefcase stowed under the seat in front of him. "Annie, why would a woman abandon her baby?"

She frowns. "Could be any of a number of reasons. I don't know."

"You're a woman." He winces as soon as the words are out of his mouth.

"That doesn't mean I know how all women think. Am I to judge all men by what you do?"

He's not sure how to interpret this and has just decided that she has insulted him when she smiles.

"Just teasing," she says.

He smiles back. "Point taken."

He busies himself by opening his briefcase and pulling out the first few pages of the manuscript. "I'd like you to read this and tell me what you think."

"All right." She takes the papers from him, puts on her reading glasses, and settles into her seat.

Paul leans back and closes his eyes. They're on the early flight. Should be in Vancouver by 9:15, connection at 9:40, in Victoria by 10:30 latest. They can put in a full day at the archives.

The part of the manuscript he gave Annie to read is a legend which sounds authentic. He'll have her research it. He has re-read it often; it's become familiar.

✧

THRICE UPON A TIME THERE WAS A WOMAN

The Indian legend says that one day a wooden box washed up on the beaches of a small village on a great sandpit (weehoo) out at sea. The box came to rest in front of the Chief's house and inside lay a girl-child wrapped in a blanket on which was woven the Eagle crest of the Larhskeek phratry. The Chief, whose daughter had recently drowned, believed that the gods had answered his pleas and returned her spirit through this strange child. He therefore adopted the baby girl whom he called Esileh, and raised her as his own, though he never told her of her origin, thus angering the spirits of her ancestors.

One day, when Esileh was sixteen, she found the Eagle blanket hidden in a copper box. Not knowing it was her own, she placed it around her shoulders, and thus unleashed the spirits that were imprisoned within the Eagle's claws. Whisperings filled her head and her limbs began to flail, so great was the anger of these spirits from the Underworld. Overcome by their power, she dropped to the ground in convulsions. The Chief heard her cries and, when he removed the Eagle cloak from around her shoulders, Esileh fell into a trance and could not be awakened. For many days she lay on her bed, growing weaker, and though the Chief summoned many halaet who used potions and dances, none could bring her back. Finally, the Chief offered sacrifices and gifts to the Eagle, and begged him to release his daughter.

And the Eagle took human form and said to the Chief, "The spirits of her ancestors will not rest until she has descended into the Underworld and lived through them the heritage you have denied her. For one cannot exist in the present without knowledge of the past."

He bade the Chief to summon his most famous carver and had her figure carved in an arm's length of yew. When the carving was ready, Esileh was lifted from her bed and laid in a corner of the house, with the carved figure over her heart. The Eagle then covered her with bear skins and began to dance and sing incantations. He implored the loon to come and take her to the Underworld. After three days, there began labored breathing under the bear skins and when the Eagle lifted the top one, he found only the carved figure. He covered it once again and, secure in the knowledge that the loon had come, the Eagle continued his incantations.

When Esileh awoke from her trance, she was no longer in her father's house. She was standing by the water's edge, and a loon spoke softly from below. "Take hold of my feet and I will dive into the water to the Underworld. And when you meet your two ancestors, Trawe'tsarual and Enireh'tac, you must trick them and enter their bodies. You may live in each for six days only. If you do not leave then, you shall be trapped forever in the Underworld."

So saying, the loon dove into the water, and Esileh was taken down to the bottom of the sea, where a cavern opened into a long dark passage. When they had swum its length, Esileh found herself on a sunny beach, at the mouth of a river. A young girl sat sobbing at the river bank. Esileh asked, "Who are you and why do you cry?"

"I am Trawe'tsarual. And though I am destined to be alone, I long to bear a child."

And when Esileh knew that this was one of her ancestors, she became a sigh and thus entered the young woman on her breath. Trawe'tsarual began to sing a lament meant to summon Woman-of-the-Sea. And when she appeared, Trawe'tsarual begged her to capture the ebb-tide so that her menses would stop. "I will give you anything you wish in exchange," she said.

Woman-of-the-Sea answered her, "I want no earthly things. You shall have a girl-child but when she comes of age, my son will claim her though she lives in her husband's house." Trawe'tsarual agreed and Woman-of-the-Sea said, "Take off your copper bracelets and give them to me. They shall return to you when your child is born."

And Trawe'tsarual slipped the bracelets off her wrists, and with them Woman-of-the-Sea imprisoned the ebb-tide.

Now without the tides to roll back the water, clams and shellfish remained buried in the sea and the villagers grew poor and hungry. The bravest among them went out in a canoe and lanced a shark which he brought to shore. He then skinned it, and when the hide had dried, he pulled it over his head and became a shark. So, in Trawe'tsarual's seventh month, the shark swam out to sea and with his fin, removed the bracelets around the ebb-tide. Loose, it rushed to shore, washing the bracelets onto the sand. Trawe'tsarual began her labor. "Quick," said the loon to Esileh, "come out now for your six days are over." And as Esileh took her human form, Trawe'tsarual died and left behind a baby girl called Enirch'tuc. "Take the bracelets," the loon instructed, "and put them round your wrists." Esileh pushed the copper bracelets over her hands and once again took hold of the loon's feet. They traveled back up through the dark passage, and when they were once more on the water between worlds, the loon called a blackfish and made Esileh lie on its back and rest. "Tomorrow we'll go back," the loon said. "Now you must restore your strength."

And in her house, the Eagle still sang his incantations and in her *place still remained only the carved figure.*

Early the next morning, the loon awakened her and took her once more below the sea. And when they reached the same river bank again, a young girl sobbed among the stones. And Esileh said, "Who are you and why do you cry?"

"I am Enireh'tac. And I have taken a lover who will not reveal himself."

And when Esileh knew that this was the second of her ancestors, she became a tear and slipped into the young woman's mouth. As darkness fell, Enireh'tac left her husband's bed and went to meet her lover, Le'inah'tan. And when he was beside her, she asked as she had every night, "Will you not reveal yourself to me?"

But Le'inah'tan shook his head and warned her, "If you should see me, I would die." Each morning, Enireh'tac awakened in her husband's bed. Le'inah'tan was gone and in front of her house lay the carcasses of sea-lions, whales, or sharks. And her husband grew wealthy, being able to trade the meat for other riches.

One morning, Esileh heard the loon's whisper, "Tomorrow you must leave for it is the sixth day." But Esileh had fallen in love with Le'inah'tan and she now wanted him for herself. The next morning, when Le'inah'tan crept from her bed, Esileh took her human form and followed him. And as he reached the water's edge, he became transformed into a huge grizzly bear with a dorsal fin on his back. Ignoring his warning, Esileh embraced him and begged him to come with her to the world above. But Le'inah'tan shook his head, then slowly began to sing his dirge. And as he sang, his form became increasingly rounded and small, until he turned into a smooth flat pebble at her feet. Esileh sank to her knees and began to sob. "Take the stone. We must move quickly," the loon said at her side. Esileh pocketed the stone and once again grasped the loon's feet. Soon they were back on the surface between worlds. She had lived two lifetimes in twelve days. The loon summoned the blackfish and Esileh lay down and rested.

When she awakened, the loon said, "And now in order to return to your house, you must throw the stone and bracelets back to the sea.

Quickly, because there is not much time left."

But Esileh, bewitched by Le'inah'tan, refused to part with the stone. "He belongs to the Underworld," the loon said. "You must throw back these tokens, because though thus far they have served as amulets, they will now turn against you and trap you forever in this world in between."

Esileh refused, and as the moments passed, the loon began to fade and soon he became one of the crests of the waves.

Esileh rode the blackfish and sang love songs to woo Le'inah'tan, until she became weak with hunger and thirst, but he did not show himself. Finally, when she knew she was dying, she threw the stone into the sea and from it sprang an island green with meadows and forests. The blackfish dropped her on a sandy beach and salmon came to rest at her feet. When her strength returned, she took off her bracelets and threw them across the sand, and in their place, mountains arose with waterfalls and streams. And Esileh's spirit was destined to roam the island and, at each river bank, take human form for six days.

She still lives on, and if a fisherman comes upon the island by chance and hears her song, he turns his back, because it is believed that anyone who sets eyes on the woman of the island becomes trapped forever in that middle world.

❖

Victoria, B.C.
May 10, 1987

Detective Paul Evans
RCMP Detachment
Prince Rupert, B.C.

Dear Detective Evans:

I received your letter yesterday. It seems a fantastic coincidence. The names you mentioned do, in fact, belong in my family but as to their stories, I'm afraid I would be of little help. My mother, Catherine Andrews, and I left Prince Rupert when I was still a boy. I'm afraid I know little about my father that you don't already know, and even less about my mother's life before she married. As to my descendants, I'm sorry to disappoint you on this account. My wife and I had a daughter, Helen, who passed away twenty-six years ago. There is no one else.

I am curious about the manuscript you mentioned and also about its author. I am not in a condition to travel — my health has not been good these past few years — but I would appreciate it if you could take the time to see me when you are next in the lower mainland.

I thank you in advance.

Sincerely yours,

Timothy Andrews

Paul Evans
RCMP Detachment
Prince Rupert, B.C.

May 15, 1987

Mr. Timothy Andrews
Saguanay House
Victoria, B.C.

Dear Mr. Andrews:

Thank you for your prompt reply.
I am enclosing a copy of the manuscript. Perhaps you would be so kind as to read it and let me know how accurate you deem it to be. If you remember anything else that might aid me in identifying the young woman, please call me collect.
Until I hear from you,

                      Sincerely yours,

                      Paul Evans

Encl.

SUBTEXT:
The History of Laura and Henry

April 11, 1987.

It's ironic how all this has turned out. What began as a search for roots has ended as an imitation of ancestral history. Even now I can't be sure which came first.

Four years ago, two major incidents: a car crash which killed both my parents; and a letter addressed to me to be opened on the event of their death which told that I was adopted. I found myself suddenly without family. A displaced person. The only clues to my identity were contained in a bentwood box given to me by my parents' lawyer. Inside were letters and notes made by my great-grandmother, Catherine Andrews. Perhaps the subsequent search through the past was simply a defence against grief, a need to find a connection, a justification for the present.

I used to believe man had volition, but now, increasingly so, I realize how wrong this is. I have been thinking about intimacy. That one elusive word which forms the link between two human beings; the word which connotes knowledge. *But does one person ever really know another? Thoughts struggle in my head, alone, neither transferable nor communicable. Perhaps writing them down is the closest I will come to being intimate with someone — a stranger who, in my words, may recognize something of himself. But even this is an illusion. Once written down, these thoughts are no longer mine, they are no longer what I am thinking. And so, I realize more and more that the present is simply an ongoing montage of what instantly becomes the past. And the past is only seen through hindsight; one can't change events.*

I have no power over my present. It simply happens to me. Catastrophic as the changes in my body. I no longer anticipate anything. There is no future either — there is only the present waiting to happen, waiting to become the past.

I have lost my sense of consequence. Cannot priorize myself into a set of values. What do values matter in the inevitability of cycles?

I was adopted as a baby. My natural mother killed herself, her grandmother abandoned a baby, and her great-grandmother died in childbirth. We are women with an hereditary gene which makes us unable to mother. I have given my baby up.

We are strong women who love meek men with no convictions. Perhaps it is their vulnerability that we love; their weakness that makes us more powerful. We strive for independence, for autonomy, tell ourselves this is happiness, this is equality, this is power. Yet all the while, we yearn for that one man whom we could regard as equal; for that one man to whom we could tell our thoughts and have them understood.

But this is mere theory — the romantic fantasy of a nineteenth-century novel. The man we seek to complete ourselves is too much like us, too afraid to risk himself in the telling of his dreams.

I've been unable to gain much information about my natural mother, other than her name. Recent history is the hardest to obtain, carefully guarded by all levels of government.

Catherine, too, never knew her parents. I have pieced together their history as it may have happened.

It has been difficult to interpret the past. Vital links are missing. There is no conclusive evidence of Laura's and Henry's existence, other than as names in records. Yet I know them to be my great-great grandparents.

The archives bulge with a mosaic of historical data, personal accounts, poems, songs, and photographs — all evocative — an invitation to invention.

The baby's name is Gitrhawn.

Henry

1. *Poem by Anne McCrae, 1962*

"Gold in the Cariboo!"
The cry ignites a rhapsody of men
bridges language, customs, continents
in a delirium of kilts, fiddles, pipes,
pictures and tales of native lands.

Gamblers, miners, dreamers,
prospectors from San Francisco
filled with renewed greed;
low-slung revolvers, Derringers
picks, spades and beans.

Magnetic, this golden force
drags weary bodies through wilderness
on mules, on horseback, on foot,
to scale rocky terrain,
cling to the sheer glisten of a cliff face
crawl over single logs
hundreds of feet above
the churning muddy currents
of the Fraser — a frigid tomb.

And in the solemn orchestral movement
men whittle forests
into cabins, sluice boxes, wagons, coffins;
slash through the wilderness
tidal boars
leaving a wake of settlements, towns, ranches, farms.

These are heroic sounds,
history peopled with the histrionics of success;
for each such hero, fifty paupers died
golden fingers pointing
a slow deliberate suicide.

2. *Photograph 1:*

> September 1860. In the foreground, a ship docked in Victoria Harbour. Men disembarking, packs slung over their shoulders. In the background, the bluish mass of distant mountains, jagged cliffs and silhouettes of islands jutting into the lightening sky, and gnarled rocky ridges like long mossy fingers pointing into the sea. In the right-hand corner, a young man is captured in shadow, facing the ship.

His name is Henry and he is shivering in the rain, relieved to be standing on land. He's been seasick through most of the three-month voyage from England.

Five years ago, his father went to San Francisco. Since then, his mother's death, a letter to his father, months of waiting in between. Henry stands on the dock in Victoria and watches the ship's unloading. The rain trickles into his collar and down his neck, but he continues to face the ship.

"You!" A man's voice beside him. "Town's up that way. Just follow the rest. You'll drown if you stand there much longer."

Henry sighs; picks up the cloth bag at his feet. He turns his back on the ship and begins to follow in the line of men leaving the dock. His father will be waiting at the Oriental Hotel.

He walks, aware of the din around him: men's shouts, horses' hoofs, the clang of a blacksmith's hammer, the hollow resonance of boots on wooden boardwalks — sounds which begin to stir him. He laughs, pushes the wet hair out of his eyes, wondering if he will recognize his father.

The Oriental Hotel is a rickety rooming house. Everything here is built of wood. Not at all like the grand hotels in London. He carefully avoids the horse dung caked onto the third step and goes inside. In the small, crowded lobby, Henry waits for his eyes to adjust to the dense dusk and the thick of cigar smoke which clings to the air and turns everything a greyish blue. He searches among the faces for his father, then goes to the rolltop oak desk to the left of the staircase.

"Mr. Stewart's room number, please."

The clerk behind the desk looks lazily through the register, then back at him. "You Henry?" he asks.

"Yes."

"You're to go see Jake Calder. Over there." He points to a group of men near the one small window in the room. "He's the tallest one of the lot."

"Thank you." Henry hesitates, swallowing a couple of times before walking towards the men near the window.

They stop talking when he reaches them, and stare at him. Jake Calder is slightly taller than Henry's six feet, but so broad across the chest and shoulders that Henry feels small by comparison. He hides his long thin fingers in the folds of his bag. Jake nods to the men and, as if by a pre-arranged signal, they silently turn and leave them alone.

"Come, sit down," Jake says. "You must be tired after your trip."

Henry smiles. Jake's face is tanned and his hazel eyes do not return the smile. He draws two chairs close together and abruptly motions Henry into one.

"I don't know how to tell you this." Jake combs a hand

over his forehead, into his hairline.

"Where's my father?"

"I'm sorry I have to be the one to tell you," Jake says. "Thing is, we ran into some trouble on the way here and Stew — your father . . . well, he didn't make it."

"What do you mean?" Henry leans forward. His hands feel suddenly cold and he rubs them one against the other.

"Like I said, there was trouble. A shooting." Jake pauses and looks down at his boots. "He got buried proper, though. I saw to it myself."

Henry sits still, the cold spreading from his hands into his entire body. He swallows; can't say anything.

Jake pats his shoulder. "I've got your father's pack upstairs. Some mining gear and a little money. I reckon you can join up with us. We'll be heading out tomorrow." He stands up. "Come. I'll show you the room. You'll need to get some rest." Jake takes his arm; coaxes him out of the chair.

Henry follows. The noise of the room is a whirring, deafening sound. He fights the impulse to cover his ears. Jake takes him to a room on the second floor and leaves quietly. Henry lies on the bed, fully clothed, and cries himself to sleep.

They cross to the mainland, to New Westminster, the next afternoon, in a boat Henry is certain is not sea-worthy.

"Here, have a swig of this," one of the men says, passing him a bottle of whiskey. "I'm sorry about your Pa."

Henry tilts the bottle back and swallows. A pleasant taste, he thinks, feeling the burn all the way to his stomach. He takes another drink before passing the bottle back.

The men settle below to play poker — the easiest way to spend time and money here.

After they leave, Henry sits on the deck and stares at the passing island shores. A raven procession. His mother's funeral. There are memories he doesn't allow himself to have. Sometimes in sleep, the past replays in dreams more vivid than reality.

Brutal beatings. His mother's face disfigured. The long knife wound under his ribs. As long as he can remember, his father's presence at home always left permanent scars.

3. *Photograph 2:*

The Fraser River, turbulent grey, cuts through sheer cliff faces. A narrow path dissects the serrated embankments of the canyon; winds a perilous trail to the edges.

If you stare hard enough, you can see the slash of an axe in rock, or the corduroy lanes with gaps large enough for a leg.

Men are huddled around a campfire high above the Fraser River.

Henry crouches in the darkness. His feet ache. His stomach grumbles. The smell of beans draws him closer to the fire. They've stopped for a few minutes only three times all day. Today's rain has turned the earth to mud which cakes onto their boots and splashes half-way up their thighs. Henry wishes he'd never come as he shivers near the burning coals. Sometimes, it takes a half hour to stop his teeth chattering. He remembers his mother coughing under a mound of blankets.

"Could you pass that bottle over?" he asks Jake. "I'm frozen solid."

"Don't get too used to that," Jake says, but passes him the bottle.

Henry shrugs, takes two large mouthfuls, feels better. He moves closer to the fire and stares into the darkness. The forest is alive. Dark, branches advancing. He shuts his eyes. He has had too much whiskey. When he re-opens them, he sees elongated shadows. "What's that?"

"Don't move." Jake's voice.

Seven Indians circle them, one for one. Henry holds his breath, waits out the tension in the silence. One hand nervously rubs the butt of his gun.

Two of the Indians move towards the pot, motioning.

"They want the beans," Jake says, his voice even and loud.

"Over my dead body." The miner next to him pushes hard against one of the Indians. "Go on. Get out of here."

Henry watches as the other miners draw guns and force the Indians to retreat towards the river.

He hesitates, then points his gun at the figure nearest him, but the Indian stares back, motionless.

"Get away from there," he shouts. "You've no right to take our food." He waves the gun, motioning the Indian away and hears Jake say, "Easy, Henry. Easy now."

He keeps the gun aimed. "You're no better than my father," he says, throat tight.

"Give me the gun, Henry." Jake is at his elbow.

"Think you can take food out of our mouths."

"The gun, Henry."

"You killed her, you did. As sure as if you'd pulled the trigger." He is staring into the Indian's face, but sees only his father. His palm is wet and slides around the butt. He shifts the gun to his other hand and wipes the sweat on his trousers.

Before he can stop him, the young Indian reaches the pot, spits inside, then runs towards the river. Henry raises his gun and pulls the trigger.

He isn't ready for the sound, nor for the sight of the boy's body flying through the air into the darkness below. "I came to kill him," he says dully. "Only someone beat me to it."

They dump the beans quickly, break camp, and hide in the woods, fearing reprisal. The men want to leave Henry behind, but Jake confiscates his gun and swears to be responsible for him. In the darkness, they steal to the land above Soda Creek.

November 1860. They arrive in Keithley to five feet of snow. Here, the party splits into three groups — Jake suggests he and Henry form a partnership.

"I don't know anything about mining," Henry says. "Why would you want me for your partner?"

"You're young, strong. I'll make a miner out of you in no time."

Henry has nowhere else to go. He planned his father's murder after his mother died. Every detail, every word he would say. He rehearsed it so often while waiting for the letter, then later on the ship, that sometimes now he thinks of it as something that happened, a distant memory. He caresses the knife in its sheath — the same one his father used years before.

Henry assumes his father's character; Jake a collusive partner in the transformation.

There is truth, perhaps, in what psychologists say. People recreate the problematic aspects of their past, preferring what is familiar above all else. Discernible patterns which exist through generations, meticulously re-enacted to the same end.

January, 1986.

I was reading text copied from the Archives. Trying to find names, dates, validation. Marc came into the study, asked me to tell him what I'd found. I could only shake my head.

Often, he sits on the rug of my study and tells me stories about himself. Only the truth, he says, implying much more. He is compelled to reveal in minute detail the incidents that have shaped him. I listen to his past, to that transfusion of context which he hopes will bond me to him, unable to disclose mine. My past is a mutating mass of collective memory. Or amnesia.

Some nights I awake from dreams to the heavy sweep of hunger in Marc's arms. I have been leaving him so long I have forgotten I'm still here. In the dark, he strokes my ribs like a blind man touching the ridges of a Victorian poison bottle.

4. *Personal Account by J.D. Russell.*

A story about Antler Creek and the four men who laid the first claims. Two returned to Keithley for supplies: Doc Keithley (the town's namesake) and George Weaver. They were followed back to the creek by men determined to stake a future:

"I remember that night, it was so cold, the hair in our nostrils froze. We had to walk slow 'cause of the snow and the packs. We was all packing near a hundred pounds of supplies — flour for bannock, dried fruit, beans, rice, tea, sugar, salt, tarps for shelter, bedrolls, an axe, a pick, a shovel, gold pans, and guns.

So we trudged up Keithley Creek five miles, then went off northeast, up a narrow ravine, always being careful to stay enough behind Doc and George so as they wouldn't know we was following.

Finally we come up to Snowshoe Creek, then trailed it seven miles. At last we stopped to rest for a while. We could see all around: above us, a plateau; north and east, great rugged mountains; and below, rolling hills, plateaus, and ravines with so many creeks through them, looked like we were seeing a map.

We waited till Doc and George started up again. Downhill this time. The path was slippery, and we moved quicker on account of the heavy packs on our backs. We come across windfalls and sometimes cliffs we didn't expect.

Finally, up ahead we seen a creek winding up the middle of a narrow valley. All around there was hills going down to flats and benches of clay and gravel deposits.

We heard the men talking up ahead, and stopped. Then suddenly Doc calls out, 'This is it, boys. Stake your claims.' You never seen so many men come out all at once. The woods was full of them.''

Henry and Jake struggle to reload the packs onto their shoulders, then slip and slide on the snow newly packed smooth by men's feet.

Suddenly, Jake loses his balance and falls down a steep embankment.

"Goddamn."

Henry leans over the edge and pulls on Jake's arm. "Are you all right?"

"Goddamn," Jake says again. "Must have turned my ankle. I better rest it a minute."

Henry sits down on the bank. He looks at Jake's foot which lies in the snow at an odd angle. "You sure it isn't broken?" he says. "Let me help you off with the pack."

"No. You go on ahead and stake for us," Jake says. "I'll

rest a minute and follow."

Henry hesitates. "I can't leave you here."

"I'll be all right. Just go. Before it's all staked out."

Henry makes the short descent to the creek. The Keithley party has already staked a great portion of the creek, and by now the men who were behind them have laid claims to the adjoining areas. Henry walks quickly past them. Some have already unloaded their packs and begun panning. Henry knows very little about staking. He's been relying on Jake to teach him.

He walks a quarter mile before he finally reaches the end of the long string of men who have claimed before him. He sets down his pack and watches the two men closest to him scramble on the limestone sides of the creek. He is surprised that the creek is not frozen, given the snow and icy temperature. He supposes it takes longer to freeze swiftly-moving water.

He has to ask instructions on how to stake a claim, then follows the example of the men around him.

On the waterworn bedrock, he finds an exposed pocket of gold, rusty in color because of the oxidized iron around it. He reaches down and pulls out a nugget about two inches in diameter. His shout mingles with those of others. He looks up the creek, to see if Jake is coming. What can be keeping him? He shrugs, then pulls from his pocket a small dark-blue leather pouch. It belonged to his father. His mother stitched it herself and gave it to him for good luck when he left. Henry places the gold nugget inside, then continues to search in the banks until the hills on either side of the creek cast dark shadows.

He hasn't realized how late it is. The two men next to him have begun to make camp for the night.

"Jake?" he calls, looking up the creek. He sees scattered fires and men moving around them. After pocketing the leather pouch, he begins to walk quickly beside the bank, calling Jake's name.

He finds him a few feet from where he left him. Jake has fallen a little lower on the slope and now lies motionless on his side in the snow, the pack still slung to his back. His eyes are closed.

"Jake! Jake wake up!" Henry slaps his friend's cheeks lightly. They are cool to the touch and Jake's eyelashes are filled with ice crystals.

In the dusk, Henry can see Jake's hands bluish in the snow and his gloves half-buried a few feet away. Henry gently removes the pack, then sits in the snow and lifts his friend's upper body against him. Jake's breath is coming out in tiny spurts of steam against his coat. "Oh God, let him be all right," he whispers. He takes Jake's hands and rubs snow against them gently and quickly. Jake told him that this is the way to fight frostbite. Soon, he begins to see pink under the surface and he raises the hands to his mouth, blowing warm breath into the fingers. He puts his own gloves around Jake's hands, then begins to vigorously rub his legs. Jake's breathing deepens; larger clouds of steam escape from his open mouth.

"I'll go and get help. We've got to carry you down to a campfire before you freeze solid."

Two miners from the adjacent claim help Henry carry Jake down in a blanket, then build him a shelter out of dead wood and branches. Henry keeps a fire going through the night and the next day, but Jake begins to cough and his temperature rises. Henry sits beside him, thinking about his mother. By the end of the second night, he knows he has to get Jake to a doctor back in Keithley Creek.

He can't do it alone. He asks for help but the men, filled with a fever of a different kind, don't want to leave the creek so soon. In the last two days, more men have arrived, and all are digging greedily, some well into the night with the aid of lanterns.

Unable to find any other way, Henry offers to give his and

Jake's claim to any new arrivals who will make the trip back with them. He keeps only the gold in the blue leather pouch.

Three men make the journey back with him so that they are able to take turns carrying the stretcher fashioned out of two wooden poles and a blanket doubled over for strength between them. Although Jake is bundled in several blankets Henry has borrowed, he continues to cough and shiver. Henry can't decide if it is better to keep moving or to stop and build a fire to try and warm Jake whose fever continues to rise. He packs snow between the folds of his scarf, then applies it to Jake's forehead. When they stop, he boils water from the creeks and makes strong tea which he has to pour into Jake drop by drop.

It takes them three days to reach Keithley Creek. The doctor diagnoses Jake's cough as mild pneumonia.

Henry takes a hotel room and sits by Jake's bed, nursing him with the medicines the doctor has given him.

His mother's illness lasted three weeks. There was no money for medicines. Henry could not stop the violent trembling under the blankets. He watched her frail body mime a desperate dialogue, and listened to the diminishing breaths until there was silence and stillness — until the room swelled with her absence and his emptiness. It was then he'd written his father.

"He's out of danger," the doctor tells Henry at the end of the second week. "But he'll be weak for a while. Don't let him get up or move about, and keep him warm and full of medicine."

Henry uses up most of the gold he panned on that first day to pay for the doctor, the medicines, and their living expenses.

By the time Jake is well enough to return to Antler Creek in early February, four hundred men have staked claims along a mile and a half of the creek. Henry and Jake stake a new claim, but this one yields little more than expense money. Supplies, though now available in Antler Creek, are costly.

Whereas other miners have credit or backers, neither Henry

nor Jake have anything to put up as collateral for a loan. By late April of 1861, discouraged and broke, they sell their claim and return to Keithley.

✧

February 1986.

Marc says, "Why do you have to make Henry such a weak character? Why can't he be powerful and wealthy?"

"Destiny," I say.

"What has destiny to do with this? You're the one manipulating him."

Can anyone, in fact, avoid a predetermined path? Like tricking the three Fates: Clotho who spins life's gossamers into a tweed of radiance and shadow; Lachesis who twists the thread, stretches out weaknesses and mats strengths; Atropos who with her shears can sever a lifetime. And all three women, these mythical creatures who preside over our futures.

✧

5. Victoria *Daily Colonist*, Dec. 10, 1933

"William's Creek," as it was originally named, was discovered by a party consisting of Michael Costin Brown, another Irishman named Costello, and "Dutch Bill" Diez.

Mr. Brown, the last survivor of the discovery party related the story of the occurrence while resident in Victoria in his old age:

"While we (Brown and Costin) were at Antler Creek, two men came into our camp, William Diez, familiarly known as 'Dutch Bill,' and Mike Burns. They had been prospecting the neighboring country . . . Dutch Bill seemed anxious to continue prospecting and offered to join us. This offer was accepted . . . We traveled down the stream, and came to a place near a little gulch or canyon where we camped for the night, building a brush shelter.

On the following morning, we separated to prospect the stream, agreeing to meet again at night to report progress.

The story of that day's prospectings, which we recalled over the camp fire, has become a matter of mining history in British Columbia. Dutch Bill made the best prospect, striking pay dirt worth a dollar or so a pan. You can well imagine we were well pleased with our day's exertions and each man felt we had at last discovered rich ground."

May 1861. A hotel room in Keithley Creek. "Our luck hasn't run out yet," Jake tells Henry. "Antler Creek is *nothing* compared to Williams Creek."

Henry looks up. He is sitting, elbows leaned on the small table, his chin cupped in one hand, a glass of whiskey in the other. He stares, unfocused, at the liquid in the glass. Gold swirling against the sides — like waves against a shore. Both of them make him sick. He looks at Jake, marveling at his optimism. How can he go on dreaming and planning?

"How old are you, Jake?" he asks.

"Twenty-six. What's that to do with anything?"

"Nothing. Nothing." Henry sighs and sips a little whiskey. "How long have you been mining?"

"Prospecting."

"Sure, prospecting. How long?"

"Since I was sixteen, seventeen." He shrugs.

Henry begins to move his glass in a circular pattern on the table, his eyes staring at the whiskey which splashes against the sides. He sighs again.

"Have you been listening to what I said?" Jake shakes his shoulder.

"Sure, I heard."

"Well, don't you want to know *how*?"

Henry nods. He lays his glass down and crosses his arms. He wants Jake's words to be true. He's been working at *Red-Headed Davis'* store the past month. It's not a lot of money but it's more than Jake makes panning their small claim on Keithley Creek. They've been saving, trying to get enough together so when the time is right, they can buy more supplies and tools.

"How much money have we got?" Henry asks.

"Enough to go with. If we don't try every chance we get, we're never going to get anywhere." He pauses. "I just feel it in here," he says, his index finger tapping his temple. "This time we're gonna make it."

They leave in late May, following the same route to Antler Creek, then continue up the creek to a small stream. The trail is well marked; they follow muddy snowprints and climb a mountain slope to the right of the creek, until they reach a broad plateau devoid of trees. A mile below them, Williams Creek winds through a narrow valley.

6. *Williams Creek*

Scurvy common enough
on Williams Creek.
Raw swollen gums,
veins turgid with blood
as if the heart is flooded;
the creek in spring
spills like a burst of tears,
flows a river down Main Street.

Henry is anchored in bed
naked and still
suffering the hands of an old homoepathist
who swaddles wet cloths on the limbs,
cold water quackery.
No old man can rinse the ache
the sweat of failure;
he heals when the vegetables come from Victoria
green miracles,
nature a murderous healer.

Six weeks later he's back in the bars,
back in the shafts
where water is common as fear
and laughter the color of loneliness;
and when he hobbles into town
men slap him on the back
for this small victory.

Anstead the quack is a doctor, a preacher,
a brickmaker, a farmer;
Anstead the quack is anyone you like,
if you have the money.

Anstead the quack spins enough yarns
to knit a thousand mantles round the earth.
On Williams Creek, he tells the hunger tales:

> Six days without food
> weakened to the point of death,
> clutches his sides, rolls his eyes
> my body devouring itself,
> near blind and deaf.
> Providence intervened.
> [A pause. Dramatic effect.]
> Then two dogs, rabid, fighting for a bone.
> I hurled myself between them
> (large as ponies they were)
> and snatched the bone
> sucked out the marrow
> while the two dogs growled
> with teeth close enough to quarter me.

The heartiest meal of my life,
Anstead says.

> And then the next meal, two weeks hence,
> two men this time,
> quarreling in a bakery doorway.
> One threw a pie
> the other ducked.
> I caught it,

Anstead says,
sounding like someone on TV
decades later.
So Henry gets better
Anstead talks on

isn't much to do but soak up time
while water surges from subterranean springs
up to the lip of hard-dug shafts
black and treacherous as night
nobody ever died of thirst
on Williams Creek.

Still men arrive, these Argonauts
searching the Golden Fleece
the Fraser filled with Symplegades
those floating rocks which crash together
and ground to powder everything caught between.
Some perish; some overcome

embarking on an odyssey
of lesser evils,
just as deadly

in a country where men banter guns
easy as words,
where thieving is common as colds,
murder a justifiable deed,
and justice determined by weight —
a saddle-bag carries enough
for an eight-hour head start;
where home is bare ground, tent, log hut,
and bed a chilled body, wet clothes
wrapped in a blanket of rough wool;
stiffness coaxed from the marrow
by twelve miles in the morning;

where food is scarce,
stories plenty
and disillusionment
an incurable cancer of the spirit.

In the claims around them, other miners have begun to take out gold. Some have sunk holes or shafts into the earth. Henry and Jake drive open cuts straight into the banks of the creek. They use a long-tom sluice, then pan down the black sand and concentrates lodged against the riffles. Their pans yield four to five dollars worth of gold. Hardly enough for expenses.

"Is this what we worked a month for? We built all this and now there's no gold." Henry gets up and walks to the cabin without waiting for Jake's reply. He needs a drink. He has no more whiskey; has gone without it for the last two weeks. He finds an empty tobacco tin, returns to the creek bank, and empties the bit of gold into the tin. "I'm going up yonder to see how they're doing." He nods towards the claim adjacent to theirs. He can see a large bonfire and hear the laughter of men.

"It's too soon," Jake says. "Most of the real findings are down eight, ten feet."

"And when we dig that deep, you'll be saying they're twenty feet below. I don't think you know anything about mining, Jake Calder. I'll bet you don't know any more than I do, for all your bloody stories. And all your San Francisco gold. Why'd you leave there anyway, if you were doing so well?" Henry thrusts his hands deep into his pockets, his right hand stroking the tin which contains the bits of precious metal. He waits for Jake to say something, to contradict him. He needs a drink. Perhaps this useless bit of gold in his pocket will buy him one.

Jake gets up slowly, picks up the lantern and walks towards the cabin, pan in hand.

Henry settles into a routine. He works the daylight hours and drinks his earnings at night. He has not apologized to Jake, who now doesn't speak to him except when he has to, like when Henry can't keep the water flowing evenly down the sluice, or when the riffles are full and have to be emptied. They work in silence, and at the end of the day Jake returns to the cabin, and falls asleep quickly.

As they dig deeper, their findings double, then triple. Still, Henry can't find the words to say he's sorry. He watches Jake's tin slowly fill with gold, while his own empties into his belly.

In late July, Jake says, "The way I see it, this hasn't turned out to be a partnership like it started."

Henry sits on his cot. "We've both been working the claim."

"True enough. But now we're running low on supplies. We gotta take a trip to Antler or, better yet, Keithley — we'd get better value there."

Henry knows what Jake is saying. He has no money and no gold. "Look, Jake," he says. "If you front the money, I'll pay it back. Every cent." He stands up, takes his tin out of his pocket, and sets it in front of Jake. "There. You take it. From now on, you take it all till we're square."

Jake pushes the tin away.

"I'll quit drinking, Jake. Honest, I will. It's just this damn country's gotten to me." He combs his hands through his hair. It feels sticky and dirty. "Jake, would you give me one more chance?" He sits down on the cot again and drops his head into his hands.

Jake lies on the cot and closes his eyes. "We'll see," he says quietly. "We'll see how things go the next few days."

Two weeks later, a little upstream, the Jourdan claim hits bedrock and takes out fifty ounces in nuggets.

Henry and Jake dig feverishly to the same level. Although their claim is not as rich as Jourdan's they take out twenty-three ounces of gold the first week. They work late in the night, steadily filling their packs. Soon, they have too much gold to leave unattended, and begin taking it with them to the workings each day and returning with it at night.

7. *Photograph 3:*

The inside of a miner's cabin. Two men lie huddled in cots under blankets. A third kneels in the centre of the room, holding up the edge of a floor plank.

Henry is awakened by floorplanks creaking. The intruder is a dark mass shifting in the room. Crouched in bed, Henry intuits the shadow's contours; slides the knife from beneath his pillow. He is back in England, waiting in a darkened alley outside a drinking house. At home, his mother sleeps, ill and hungry. His heart begins to pound, his stomach churning a familiar swirl. He springs, surprises the intruder, and sinks the knife into his side.

The tin of gold falls to the ground in dull clanks across the wooden floor.

"What the hell is going on?" Jake lights a match, then the lamp.

Henry feels the staggering weight against him; lies the stranger down gently.

"What have you done?" Jake bends over the man. Gold dust and nuggets rainbow across the planks mixing with blood pooling between the ridges. Henry slowly sits on the bed and watches, dispassionate, as Jake tries to revive the man.

He has seen many huddled bodies in alleys. How else to survive? He didn't question it then and doesn't now.

"He's going to die," Jake says, turning to him. "Why didn't you shout? He'd have run scared."

Henry shakes his head. "I didn't think about it. I just reacted."

"You didn't think." Jake turns to him. "You've just killed a man."

"He was a thief."

Jake stares at him, then back at the floor. "We've got to get someone. Can't leave him here. Damn you." He gets up and starts to dress. Henry watches, silent. When Jake is ready, he says, "Let's get this story straight. The man attacked you with a knife. You did it in self-defence."

Henry nods. After Jake leaves, he washes the blade, then puts it back under his pillow.

Henry and Jake work until mid-September. Henry wants to winter in Victoria.

"You'll squander everything if you go down there," Jake tells him. "Why not wait another year and save up? There's plenty of time to spend it after that."

"What's the use of having money if you can't enjoy it?" Henry's tired of miners and work. He'd like to meet new people. He has money now; he might find a girl. "Why don't you come with me?" he says.

But Jake refuses to go. "Besides," he tells Henry, "if I stay, I'll be here in the spring and get a head start, soon as the snow melts."

They don't resolve their conflict, and when the first snow falls, men around them begin to leave the creek. Henry packs his things and goes to Victoria.

8. *Letter from Mrs. Corruthers to the Archives,* 1922.

"Dear Mr. _____

I'm replying to your letter to my father, Mr.
Browning, regarding information about his early
years in the Cariboo. Let me commend you on your
admirable project. There are many facts about that
time which may otherwise be forgotten. My father
is 83 years old and still speaks vividly of his
days during the goldrush. In fact, he recalls those
memories far easier than more recent ones. He is
not well enough to write you himself, but has asked
me to do so on his behalf. I'm including several
accounts of his experiences . . . . .''

[From Mr. Browning's Account #4: Winter in Victoria, 1861-62]

". . . It was the first winter after the Williams Creek find. In order to keep a claim in those days, the men were required to live on the land continuously. However, because of the snow, the Gold Commissioner gave them six-month layovers. Most men went south in early September, before the road closed.

The largest numbers converged in Victoria. Here they lived in hotels and drank and gambled until most of their money was gone. Nuggets and gold dust was acceptable currency in the saloons which kept scales behind the counters. Father was a bartender at the Oriental Hotel during that winter.

He tells a story about a young man (whose name he can't remember), tall and thin, but tough as can be. He'd made quite a name for himself as a fighter. That winter, two, three times a week, a newcomer would challenge him in the saloon. It was all legal then. The miners took sides — the regulars always bet on the young man — and he always won. He received a percentage of the bets. Father says he made more money betting on that young man than he did by bartending.

As you can imagine, with so much gold in circulation, crime was common. Not only stealing, but murders and the like. Father's housemaid was killed that winter and her murderer never found . . . ."

January 1862. It is not the life Henry envisioned in Victoria. Excepting the landscape, he could still be in the goldfields, surrounded by similar men, similar circumstances. Each day when he awakens, sober, in late afternoon, he despairs at the course he is following. In shadow with himself. It takes a few drinks to dullen the swarm of malaise.

In the midst of this, he falls in love by accident. Perhaps it is not even love, but simply an obsession more intoxicating than gold or whiskey. The girl's name is Babette; she is a housemaid to the bartender at the Oriental Hotel and a year younger than himself. She has his mother's eyes and the same hummingbird hands. When Henry tries to court her, she is soft-spoken but firm. Her master, she says, has warned her about miners. And she herself has seen the men who populate Victoria saloons in the winter. They're wealthy when they arrive and paupers when they leave. She will not marry a miner, she tells Henry. They do not make good husbands.

Henry tries to stop thinking about Babette, but her face haunts him and her words repeat themselves in his head. He decides he will show her that she's wrong. He'll be kind to her; perhaps she will fall in love with him. Within the month, he's watching her house, then following her. She neither looks nor speaks to him ever, although he's certain that she must recognize him.

One evening, he's hiding in the trees near her house when she comes out. He no longer even tries to speak to her. She walks quickly, turns her head this way and that, as if searching for someone. He keeps well behind her and hides when she turns. Suddenly, a young man emerges from the shadows towards her. They embrace, then enter a nearby house. For a while, Henry stands outside in the cold. She's no different than the women he pays, he tells himself. He's been made a fool by a servant girl. He walks back to the saloon and orders whiskey. The liquid warms him and gives him strength. He has five drinks in succession, tossing his head back and downing each in one gulp. Then, he goes back to her house and waits.

She returns a little past midnight. He hears her footsteps before he sees her and has enough time to surprise her from behind, his hand over her mouth. Her eyes stare, frightened, and for a moment, he wonders what he's doing.

Her fear arouses him, and he drags her into the shadows. She small and struggling against him; he pulling her deeper into the underbrush. There is the smell of smoke from chimneys of nearby houses, and the drone of voices from within. He tightens his grip, flattens his palm against her mouth, and pushes her to the ground. He feels dizzy. What is he doing? Let her go, he thinks, everything will be all right. A battering begins against his body — from outside and within, he can't tell which. Brambles scratch his arms, and her legs kick against him. The more she struggles, the harder he holds her. Suddenly, her teeth dig into his palm, the pain so sharp, he pulls his hand away. A scream begins in her throat and Henry can only think of stifling it. He wants everything to stop — his struggle, hers, the melancholy. He clamps his palm over her mouth once more and gropes with his other hand in the ground, until he finds a stone.

He hears the thud against her temple, feels it through his

hand, then she lies still and he remains on her, his breath so loud it frightens him. He lifts his hand from her mouth and her head falls, limp, to one side. He rolls off her. A cold sensation spreads in his stomach. He can't look at her. He stumbles up and runs through the trees until he's at the other end of the street. Then, he walks quickly back to his hotel, head down, and locks himself in his room.

When he awakens the next morning, he remains in bed, the events of the previous night both blurry and too clear. He's afraid to get up, to go out, certain that everyone will know what he's done. He sits up and holds his head in his hands. He's accustomed to the nausea, the vomiting which is now a daily ritual. He pushes his legs over the side of the bed and goes to wash.

Over the basin, he sees himself in the mirror and shudders, touching the skin on his face with his fingertips. Hot and damp. Eyes sunken into dark circles; face etched unrecognizable. He vomits into the basin.

He stays indoors till nightfall, as if he fears that sunlight will expose him. He's been pacing all afternoon and now is hungry and needs a drink. In the lobby of the hotel, he stops in front of a newspaper, reads the small head-line in one corner, "YOUNG GIRL FOUND MURDERED," then walks out into the street.

He goes to a saloon, sits with familiar men. She was right. They *are* all the same. What startles him most is that nothing has changed. He expected some talk, fear, speculation, accusations. It is as if Babette had never existed.

He begins to drink more than ever before; it helps him not to think. And when he brings women to his room, he is rough with them. Money dwindling, he settles into the familiarity of his other life, steals for survival, sleeps in the woods near the Indian settlement by day, and drinks whatever he can afford at night, constantly afraid of being caught.

[From Mr. Browning's Account #6: Smallpox Breakout. Spring 1862]

". . . Without warning in Victoria that spring, smallpox flared up among the Indians. Each day, more men and women became infected until the small Indian Hospital adjacent to the Victoria Hospital was full.

The people of Victoria had long been trying to rid themselves of the Indian settlement. The smallpox threat became a justification for expelling the Indians from the community. When the Indians refused to budge, the police set fire to their settlement and ordered the Indians out.

Father says it was a terrible time. Infected Indians took to the road, returned to their coastal settlements, spreading the disease. It nearly wiped out their population . . ."

Henry capitalizes on this development. He needs to join a traveling party to the creek. When he hears of a young couple who are planning to carry supplies to the goldfields, he tells them he is familiar with the route, and can lead them there quickly, ahead of the Indians.

Back in Keithley Creek, Henry forgets his fears — the Indians and their disease remain in the coastal villages. His experiences in Victoria fade with distance. He convinces himself he's done nothing wrong. The thing with Babette was an accident. With the little money he received as a guide, Henry rents a hotel room, then drinks and gambles until it's all gone.

June 1862. Keithley Creek. Jake has come and paid off his debts. Two packs lean against the door in the small hotel room. Jake stands between the two cots.

"You all set, Henry?"

"As set as I'm going to be." He sits on one of the cots, among the rumpled sheets, a bottle of half-drunk whiskey in his hand.

"Give me that," Jake says, taking the bottle from him. "You've had enough."

"I've had enough of this stinking country." Henry falls back into the bed. His head aches and he wants to sleep.

"Get up." Jake's voice is harsh. "I didn't come all this way to hear you complain."

"We'd have been better off never to come here in the first place." Henry sits up and, taking the bottle from the table where Jake has put it, takes a long swig.

"Christ, couldn't you have stayed sober this one night?" Jake wrestles the bottle away from him and pours it down the small sink beside the bed.

"It's the last one. Don't —"

"Get up. We've got to get started." Jake pulls him up by the arm and steadies him. "Turn around," he says, holding up Henry's pack.

Henry does as he's told; he has no energy to argue or to thank Jake. He straps on the pack, and although the weight makes his legs weak, he forces himself to stiffen his knees. He waits quietly until Jake has finished tying the other bundle over his own shoulders.

"I swear, this is the last time I go with you, Jake Calder . . ."

"Shut up."

Outside it's still dark. The half-moon shines between passing clouds. Henry can see his footsteps in the cool dewy ground. It's early summer but nights are still cold. Soon, the black flies will settle in. Henry doesn't know whether he prefers this cold to being bitten. He's managed through one summer. This one isn't going to be any different.

Jake leads the way along the familiar trail. How long ago it seems to Henry now. He was someone else then, someone he can never be again.

He makes himself walk, forcing his feet one in front of the

other although they feel heavy, and he wants to sleep. Jake continues to step brusquely in front of him, widening the gap between them.

"Face it, Jake," Henry shouts into the darkness. "We've had nothing but bad luck. Every trip pulls us down another foot. This damn country's going to bury us soon." He stops and wipes sweat off his brow with the back of his hand. Let Jake go on alone. What the hell is the hurry? Nothing's going to change. He shuts his eyes and stumbles. The pack throws him off balance. He lets himself fall into the low underbrush to his left. The cool wet drops from the leaves feel good against his ears and cheeks.

"Get up, you fool." Jake stands above him and, in the darkness, the whites of his eyes reflect the moon's light and frighten Henry. "It's you that's pushing us down in the mud. You and your damn drinking. You get up right now, or this is where we part company." He shakes Henry's shoulder. "You hear that? I mean it this time. You can go back to Keithley and drink yourself into a grave or you can walk." He turns and continues down the trail.

Henry forces himself upright. Jake's right. Jake's always right. He would have given up long ago if it weren't for Jake. He'll show him he can do it this time. He shakes loose branches and leaves off his chest and begins to walk. So they've had bad luck. No, *he's* had bad luck. He's made his own bad luck. Jake would be better off without him.

"I tell you, we're jinxed," he shouts. "Every trip something goes bad."

"Shut up and keep walking."

Henry trudges along and keeps quiet though his tongue is heavy with insults and abuses. He hates Jake's silence and would prefer a shouting match. But Jake won't let himself be provoked, and Henry is forced to swallow his hostility and let it churn with the cheap whiskey, forming a foul taste in his mouth.

"We ain't done so bad," Jake says now, turning to Henry, waiting for him to catch up. The sky is pink with dim light, in that time between night and day when it's too dark to see and too light to hide. "Half an hour more, it'll be light. We can stop for a bit then."

Henry's body aches. Too much whiskey and no sleep. Jake's been trying to set a steady pace but Henry lags behind. Three times in the last hour Jake stopped and waited for him.

"I can't walk another step," Henry mumbles. "Christ, my head hurts." But he continues to follow Jake, as if he were being pulled by an imaginary chain. The silence makes him edgy. Why doesn't Jake shout? That way he can strike back. Jake's steady, even steps in front of him contrast sharply to his own stumbling; make him feel all the more guilty.

"Hold on a minute, would you?" he calls. The sun, though not yet on the horizon, lights the underside of thin clouds layered into the sky to their left; turns them a reddish gold against the lightening sky. "You said we could rest when it got light."

"All right." Jake removes his pack, drops it on the ground to the right of the trail, then sits down and leans against it. From his pocket, he produces his plug of tobacco, unwraps it slowly and bites off the end. He chews quietly, staring into the distance.

Henry catches up and drops to the ground without removing his pack. He leans back against it and begins to snore almost immediately.

When he awakens, he can't tell how much time has passed. He still feels drowsy and tired. He opens his eyes; is stung by the sun that hovers an inch above the horizon. Jake is sitting in the same place, his face expressionless and his mouth still chewing.

"How long have I been out?"

"About an hour."

Henry sits up slowly, his shoulders and back sore, arms and neck stiff. He slips off the pack and stretches. "Lord, I feel awful."

Jake continues to chew.

"Many men back?" Henry asks after a while.

"Weather's been real bad. Elwyn's made the layover go another month — to the first of July. No big hurry to get back now."

"Who's Elwyn?"

"New Gold Commissioner. Set up in Richfield part of the time. Makes it a lot easier."

Henry yawns and leans back again, hands crossed behind his head. He hasn't had to worry about all the claim business. Jake takes care of all that for them. An extra month's extension will be hard on some men — those who have no claim and are waiting to take over ones that have been abandoned. He wonders if their luck will hold out all season. "You done anything yet?" he asks.

"Gravel's still frozen," Jake says between chews. "Can't work the sluice myself, anyway."

Henry hears the reproach in those words. "Most of the men go south for the winter," he says. "What's the point of staying here? It's still frozen, you can't mine. You said so yourself."

"Henry, I got something to tell you," Jake says.

"What's wrong? Did something happen?"

Jake shakes his head; sits quiet for a moment.

"Well, what is it?"

"You've been gone a while. Things change." Jake pauses, then speaks quickly. "Thing is, I got a woman living with me now. Built another cabin next to ours. She won't be no trouble. And you and me, we'll be just like before."

"Nothing wrong with that. A man should settle down if he finds a good woman."

"There's more. I might as well tell you now."

Henry waits while Jake pulls out the tobacco plug and chews off a new bit.

"Sadie, that's her name — well, that's what I call her for short — she's, well, she's an Indian woman. I brought her up from Quesnel Forks. She's a good woman. You'll like her."

Henry's startled; not sure how he feels about this. He hasn't paid much attention to Indian women. Some live with miners, but he's never considered those arrangements serious. He's seen many Indian prostitutes, especially in Victoria, but he hasn't paid for one. He looks at Jake, who is frowning at him. He really wants me to like his woman, Henry thinks. He makes himself smile. "If she's a good woman like you say, then I got nothing against it."

The new cabin stands thirty feet from the old one and also faces the creek. It has a window, Henry notes, with yellow and white curtains. The closer he gets, the more Henry feels uncomfortable — no, *embarrassed*. Not for himself, but for Jake. He doesn't want to meet Sadie. A *squaw*. He remembers all the crude jokes and stories the miners told about Indians. He remembers his own bragging in Victoria — and how everyone laughed and cheered when he told them he shot one in the back.

Henry sees movement in the window, then the woman comes out of the cabin to meet them. She's young, probably no more than twenty. She stares openly at him. He dislikes her immediately.

"This is Sadie," Jake says, putting his arm around her.

"How do you do?" Henry nods, without extending his hand. He doesn't want to touch her.

She also nods and continues to stare at him in the same even way. She has a broad face, large eyes and a flat nose. Her hair is pulled back into a thick black braid which hangs down her back to her waist. The top of her head leans on Jake's shoulder. Henry tries to hide his distaste. "I'm going to get some rest," he tells them. Although he accepts the arrangement, he doesn't have to like it.

[From Mr. Browning's Account #9: B.C. Emigration Society.]

". . . Several pack trains and a cattle drive arrived in Richfield in late June and with it, news of the B.C. Emigration Society. Apparently, some miners, having heard that a society in England was sending out ships of young girls to other British colonies, had asked an Anglican Minister to request a brideship be sent to Victoria. The first ship arrived the summer of 1862, and was filled with girls from orphanages or poorhouses who had no prospects of marriage in their own country. A second ship, *The Tynemouth*, was scheduled to arrive in Victoria in September. All summer, the men made plans to go south for this event. They couldn't reserve a bride, but they could be there to propose to the girls as soon as they disembarked . . . ."

Laura

My great-great grandmother. Perhaps she set in motion a pattern we've all followed. Is it genetic, this unsettling of equilibrium? Or have I fitted us all into my own imbalance? It doesn't matter. It could have happened like this.

9. *Poem by Anne McCrae, 1962*

The Brideship *Tynemouth*: September 1862

The men want women
mail-orders from England
children sending boxtops
for a new toy.

The chosen merchandise,
orphan girls, paupers
without husbands otherwise,
are boarded on the *Tynemouth* in summer
three months eclipsed below deck
stale air, a maelstrom in the belly
reach Victoria in fall.

On shore, three hundred men, six hundred eyes
await the auction
smooth trouser creases, lick fingers
set hair in place, dream silky shoulders

hot meals and mended clothes.
Rowboats land; girls walk in single file
flanked by the lusty breath of miners
anxious hands extended in proposals.
First come, first served.

Laura Browler is uncomfortably aware of the men around her; feels exposed — as if she were on show. She hugs her bundle of clothes to her chest and stares at her toes. Who will protect her here? She begins to wish she was still on the ship, or in England — anywhere but here. If only she could pray. She has found comfort in God before: when her mother died; when she's been lonely and afraid. God is fair; God is good. He will not forsake her.

"Girls, line up two-by-two, and follow me." Mrs. Robb is their chaperone.

Two files of policemen and marine officers march up and flank them. Laura stares at the ground while she walks. They begin marching towards the marine barracks where they will live until they secure either positions or husbands.

Dear God, Laura begins, *please help me in this new place —*

Suddenly, a young man pushes through the police file beside her and grasps her hand.

"Will you have me?" he asks.

She stops, startled in mid-prayer, and looks up. The young man is tall and slender, with a long narrow face, high cheekbones, and a straight thin nose — features, which although sharp, are almost feminine in their beauty. He's smiling and a little out of breath.

"I've got a claim," he adds quickly, "and a house for you to live in."

"Move along now. Don't hold up the line." Mrs. Robb pushes her palm in the small of Laura's back.

"Will you have me for your husband?" the young man asks again. He holds her hand tightly.

Laura hesitates. Perhaps this is God's will. Hasn't she asked Him for help? She looks at the young man. "Yes," she says.

Mrs. Robb forces her to move forward and the young man lets go of her hand. "I'll come and get you at the barracks," he says.

Laura hears men cheer around her. Then, as if an imaginary spring has been let loose, other men break through the files and propose to the girls.

"Move back. Make room." A marine officer advances, urges them forward. "Move on ladies. Plenty of time later."

Inside the barracks, the girls are each assigned a cot. Their trunks are carried in and placed at the foot of each cot. Mr. Graham of the Receiving Committee makes speeches to welcome them to the new land. The Reverend urges them to remember their religious duties, to pray to God for aid in fighting sin and temptation.

"My hope," he says, "is that you'll all soon become wives and mothers, because families are the foundation of any Christian society."

Laura sits quietly on her cot, head bowed, and listens to the Reverend's speech. But she has difficulty concentrating, because she's trying to remember the face of the young man she has accepted as her future husband.

Shortly after the Receiving Committee leaves, Mrs. Robb enters the barracks and hushes the girls. "Those of you who have already accepted a proposal will now come forward," she says.

Laura files out with the girls who form a small group. As each young man approaches the protective line of police officers, Mrs. Robb looks to the girls for confirmation that this is a prospective husband. If one of the girls nods, the young man is allowed through.

Laura's young man is fourth in line. She nods curtly to Mrs. Robb and waits for him to approach her.

"Henry Stewart," he says.

The ceremony is conducted the following afternoon — a group wedding. Laura stands beside Henry who holds her hand in his.

His skin is rough but warm, and when she finally looks at him, he smiles. She blushes and turns her head towards the Reverend. The ceremony is brief. Laura repeats her vows in unison with the other couples, then files out of the church.

Henry holds her elbow and asks her about the voyage. Laura senses he is as nervous as she is. She's grateful to talk about something other than herself.

By the time they return to the marine barracks, Laura no longer feels awkward. She chats shyly with Henry and asks him about their new home.

They'll travel to the Cariboo the following day. Henry explains that soon the road will close for the winter. Every day means more snow. They'll have to move quickly to be settled in their cabin before winter comes.

They spend the rest of the day walking around Victoria, eat meals in the restaurants of two different hotels, then return to the military barracks to retrieve Laura's trunk. The weather is still mild and the ground is sprinkled with leaves of different shades of reds, browns, yellows, and purples.

In early evening, they go to the hotel Henry has booked. Laura glances uneasily at the double bed, then settles in a chair near the window.

She faces a busy lighted street and can see men and women milling around, arm-in-arm, some laughing. Rectangles of light from house windows, hotels, and saloon doorways cast elongated patterns across the street and light the faces below. Laura twirls her new wedding band around her finger. She's thinking about her hurried conversation with Mrs. Robb last night. The chaperone explained what she might expect on her wedding night. She was embarrassed and stared at the ground throughout the conversation. Mrs. Robb told her about the unpleasant duty that would be expected of her as a married woman and that she would have to bear in silence.

She shivers, although the room is not cold, and crosses her arms over her chest. Henry is busy packing the remaining things for the journey. She can hear him moving around her, but she keeps staring down at the street.

"I'll give you a chance to get settled," Henry says suddenly, and Laura looks up. "I'll be back in a little while."

She nods and he smiles before going out. She supposes he's giving her privacy to undress, and gets up quickly from the chair, locks the door, then goes to the basin to wash. She puts on a flannel nightgown, takes down her hair, and combs it over her shoulders. She stares at herself in the mirror. She is a married woman now. But she doesn't look or feel any different. Finally, she unlocks the door, then climbs between the bedsheets and pulls the quilt up to her chin. Each time she hears footsteps in the hall, she yanks the quilt higher. After a long while, she falls asleep.

She's awakened by the weight of Henry's body on her, and is sickened by the smell of whiskey on his breath. She wants to push him away, but Mrs. Robb's face keeps appearing in front of her closed eyes. She's a wife now and this is her duty. Henry seems oblivious to her feelings. His hands squeeze her breasts too roughly, nails digging into her nipples. His body is rigid and she can feel his hip and pelvic bones pressing hard against hers. She makes her body limp and forces herself to think of something else. This is her duty. *Dear God, I put my trust in Thee*. Yes, she'll pray. *Dear God*. Suddenly Henry pulls up her nightgown and forces himself inside her so quickly that she cries with both pain and surprise. She clenches her hands into fists and lets the tears come. It is over in moments, and Henry falls to one side of her, one leg still across hers. She hears his harsh breathing near her ear.

"It'll get better," he mumbles in the darkness. "You'll get used to it."

She continues to cry silently after Henry begins to snore beside her. For a long time she lies motionless, afraid he might awaken. She prayed to God and thought He had answered her prayers. Mrs. Robb said a woman alone, especially in a strange country, is a woman lost. Laura now has a husband to protect her. Is this then her payment? She shudders.

It is your duty.
You'll get used to it.

She shuts her eyes and tries to sleep. If this is God's will, then she will do her duty. She mustn't question. *A woman alone.* She'll get used to it. She'll get used to it.

10. *Poem by Anne McCrae, 1962*

Brides genuflect to a merciless god
abstract as salvation
utter prayers of failure
admissions/submissions

Husbands and wives
legal tender
board river steamers
the brides stare from the rail
into the opulent eye of the Fraser
see the churning of blood
within a giant artery;
shudder at the ominous silhouettes of evergreens —
a tight net slung over mountains, hills, everything.

Rain. Large droplets splatter deck and river,
a baptismal mingling of sky and earth,
man and woman.

The women soon forget headlines in London papers
these wealthy promised men
drag them on mules, in crude wagons;
shelter, a tarpaulin filthy and ripped
warmth, a heated stone underfoot.

The rough narrow trail hugs canyon walls
corduroy lanes with gaps large enough for a leg
bridges are woven birds' nests
clinging to the face of a cliff.
They wear men's underwear, men's boots
tackle survival with a dogged spirit
as wind lashes the tarp
and rain puddles inside the wagon.

They reach Soda Creek in mid-October, about four weeks later, then board a river steamer to Quesnel Forks. A cold wind blows throughout the trip; Laura is happy to sit below deck.

"It's sixty miles to the goldfields from there," Henry tells her. "But it's just a trail. With luck, we can make it in just over two weeks. It's going to be a cold winter, this one."

"Tell me about the house," Laura asks.

Henry pushes the hair away from his forehead. "It's not really a house," he says. "It's more a — cabin."

Laura frowns. The cabins they've seen on the trip are tiny and have no windows. "How big is it?" she asks.

Henry shrugs. "Maybe ten, twelve feet square. Good enough for most people out here."

She hears the defensiveness in his words. "I'm sure it'll do just fine," she says, but she's disappointed. "What about land? Can I grow a garden?"

Henry laughs. "A garden? We're four thousand feet above sea level. You're lucky if you see two months of summer. As for the land, it's mining land. Mostly turned up gravel and rocks." His voice softens. "Maybe later on, after we take out bedrock gold, we could find a place with a bit of land. I'm sure you could grow something that doesn't need too much sun."

Laura sits quiet. She had dreams about her new home. She realizes suddenly that she's been imagining an English cottage, a vegetable garden, new clothes, and furnishings. How can she be so silly? Henry shifts beside her. She must not let him know her disappointment. She will make do with what they have and not complain. "It sounds fine," she says. "Tell me about your claim."

Henry smiles. "It's not just my claim," he says. "I've got a partner. His name's Jake. Good man. We've been together for the past two years, since I came."

"You never mentioned him before," Laura says. She thinks it curious that he hasn't. Perhaps it's better not to ask questions.

She's been learning things she doesn't want to know. She wonders how many more surprises there will be.

"No, I didn't. And there was a good reason," Henry says.

Laura waits.

"Jake, well, you couldn't find a better man than Jake. You'll really like him. But since last spring, well, things are a little cool between us. I was just waiting a bit to tell you, that's all."

"Tell me what?" Laura asks.

"It's not that I have anything against Indians, you understand—"

"Is Jake an Indian?"

"No, of course not. Indians don't have claims. At least not around our parts."

"What then?"

"Jake's living with an Indian squaw. Girl by the name of Sadie." Henry pauses. "I don't mind telling you that I don't like the situation and I don't like this Sadie. But Jake's my partner and they're living on the claim. In their own cabin. So I don't say anything about it, but I won't have anything to do with her. Do you understand?"

Laura frowns. "What's she like?"

"I don't know what she's like. I don't talk to her and I expect you won't be talking to her either."

"But Henry, how can you not like her if you don't know her?"

"I don't need to know her." Henry stares hard at Laura. "And neither do you. Do you understand?"

Laura looks away, then nods. She swallows a couple of times.

Henry reaches for her hand and she instinctively recoils. "Don't be upset," he says. "You don't know this country like I do. I'm only telling you things for your own good. There's white women up there you can be friends with."

"I'll get used to it," she says, sarcastically, but Henry doesn't answer.

It's one of the coldest winters on record. There is still a sixteen-day journey ahead, if everything goes right. They leave the wagon at Soda Creek and continue on foot. Laura's trunk is loaded onto one of the mules. She dispenses with fashion, takes off her crinoline and wears a pair of men's boots Henry bought for her. They are now ten people and seven mules. Three of the packers have remained in Soda Creek. Uncloistered, Laura walks side by side with the men, trading stories of England for those of the Cariboo.

✧

Wells, December 13.

I came to the goldfields, not in the way Laura came, because she was sixteen and knew little about human nature. I came with my perspective already tainted by imagination, by trying to understand how she might have felt. Some of this is true. It could have happened this way.

I came to the goldfields in an airplane as far as Quesnel. I'd made arrangements with someone from the hotel in Wells to pick me up.

I don't know what I thought I'd find here that I couldn't have read in books. Perhaps I came searching for essence. I'd imagined it so strongly back in Vancouver.

A man met me at the airport. "Gus," he said, taking my suitcase. "I'm from the Jack of Clubs. You the one that wrote?"

I nodded and followed him out to a pick-up truck. His skin was wrinkled, tanned, and his white hair combed straight back from the forehead, to just past his shoulders. He had a long matching beard, the end of which bobbed against his chest as he spoke.

"May as well settle in," he said, looking straight ahead. "It's a long ride. Been a lot of snow and I gotta go slow."

"Fine." It was nearing dusk and I strained to see out my window, trying to memorize everything — the height of the trees, the density of the forest. In the snow, it was as if the underbrush didn't exist, only trees growing against a white background. Gus turned on the headlights. The road was sanded and salted so that in places two ridges of black pavement showed through. The banks at either side were dirty and splattered with gravel.

"Will you tell me when we come to the old road going into Barkerville?" I asked.

"Old road went up the other way, through the mountains. Comes to Barkerville from the back."

"But I thought part of this was the same."

"A later road. First trail was like I told you."

"Is it still there?"

"Ain't nobody took it away, if that's what you mean." He laughed. "Doubt you'd find it in winter. But in the summer you can still hike it, or on horseback."

In twenty minutes, it was full dark.

"It's the mountains," Gus said. "Even in mid-summer we don't get sun long as you do down south."

"Do you live in Wells?"

"Yup. Nearby. Got a cabin in the hills."

"How cold does it get?"

"Forty, sometimes fifty below." He glanced at me. "You warm enough? I can turn up the fan."

"No, I'm fine." Outside, the snow glistened yellow in the branches of trees to the left of the road, branches which one of his badly aligned headlights illuminated with a single spotlight. I could feel warm air blowing onto my legs from the heater.

"How do you keep a cabin warm in this kind of weather?" I asked, imagining Laura and Henry.

"You don't." He laughed again. "You keep a fire going but it don't help much unless you're right next to it. And you gotta get up several times a night to stoke it. And still everything freezes. Pipes, *food. You wanna know how I keep fruit from freezing?"*

"How?"

"I sleep with it. Bet you never heard of that in the city."

I smiled, thinking of this man sleeping beside oranges, apples, and bananas. "No," I said.

"Out here, you gotta do what you gotta do."

He slowed the truck as the road began to steepen and wind. I closed my eyes for a bit, nervous of winter driving. At home, an inch can keep me indoors.

We arrived about two hours later, and I relaxed as soon as I saw lights twinkling up ahead. Gus turned off the highway up a hill, on the crest of which was the Jack of Clubs Hotel, a post office, a small food store, ("Nothing in there but potato chips and pop"), an old theatre, and a few boarded up buildings. I could see several side streets lined with houses, all of which didn't look very winterized.

He stopped the truck in front of the hotel, left the motor running, and carried my suitcase inside. I tried to ask him how much I owed him, but he waved me away, mumbling, "We'll take care of it later, don't you worry."

My room was on the second floor and overlooked the main street. I unpacked the few things I'd brought, then sat on the bed with my notes spread around me. I could hear jukebox music and the drone of voices from the bar below, the sound of which enticed me downstairs. Several men and women waved me to their table as soon as I entered, introducing themselves, all friendly. I was startled at first. In the city, high-fidelity dialogues rarely occur between strangers. We are all too well pressed to feel the diamond of a needle. These men and women laughed music and plucked the resonance of chords within me. We spoke for hours. There were no buses, no taxis, no foodstores, one coffee shop and one restaurant, both closed by ten in the evening. Barkerville was two miles away, one couldn't stay there, it was closed for the winter. There were two hundred residents, they told me, and a school which the government was trying to shut down. By the end of the evening, Bridgit had offered to take me cross-country skiing and show me Richfield; Nancy and

Joseph had invited me to dinner the following night; Steve who worked for the Parks Board in Barkerville said he would take me to the archives; and Gus, who joined us a little later, offered to drive me wherever I needed to go.

❖

They arrive in Richfield, leave the packers at the hotel, and head to the claim with two mules Henry must return as soon as they've unloaded the trunks and supplies.

Throughout the trip thus far, Laura has slowly become accustomed to the tall trees, the thick forests, the dense underbrush peeking through the snow, the shadows covering everything by early afternoon. She has welcomed the security of dusk. Now, on the last lap of their journey, she finds herself in the midst of a ravaged land. As far as she can see in every direction, the earth has been stripped of trees and underbrush. In its place are slag piles — mounds of gravel and rock, the discards of miners who dig shafts and re-route the creek, relentless in their search for gold. There are crude tents on the hill beside the creek as well as several small log cabins.

"It's like an abandoned battlefield," Laura says to Henry. "So barren and open."

"Not very pretty to a woman's eyes," he answers, and smiles. "But to a miner it's a whole different story. All this," and he waves his arm in a semi-circle, "is the product of a lot of men working. All this means there's gold." He looks at her. "A battlefield, yes. Abandoned? Well, come spring, there'll be hundreds of men coming back. You'll be wishing for it as it is now."

They stand quiet for a moment and Laura strains to hear winter birds, animals, anything alive. But there is only the faint whisper of water moving under the ice crust on the creek. She shivers, and wraps her arms tight around her chest.

"Are you cold?" Henry asks.

She shakes her head.

"Come on. We're almost there."

Henry moves past her, pulling the mules. She follows. They skirt the creek, walking carefully. The ground is uneven; sometimes littered with felled logs and rocks; other times sunken. The snow has settled into all the crevices, over the debris, so as to make the ground appear much more level than it is. Several times Laura stubs her toe or falls up to the knee in a hole.

"Look! You can see the claim now. The one with the two cabins close together." Henry points.

Laura stops and looks at the log cabins. They're as small as Henry described them. In this detail, she thinks, he's been truthful. A bluish smoke rises from the chimney of the cabin closest to them. As they approach, she can see this one has a larger window than the other.

"We're coming up to Jake's cabin now," Henry says. "Won't he be surprised to see you!" He pauses for a moment, then turns to her. "You didn't forget what I said? About the woman, I mean. Best to ignore it all."

Laura moves back a step, pretending to have lost her balance. She doesn't like Henry's face so close to hers, especially when he is telling — no, ordering her to do something she isn't sure is right.

"Come. I'll show you our cabin. Then I'll get Jake." Henry ties the mules to a nearby stump, then leads Laura to the second cabin.

She follows him inside, stepping over the door sill as if it were infected. It takes a couple of moments for her pupils to dilate in the semi-darkness, her eyes adjusted to the glare of the snow. She sees a bed and a dresser behind a crude wooden-slatted partition which divides the room in two. In the larger section are a table, two chairs, a long bench, and the wood cooking stove. A small curtainless window faces the creek.

"Well? What do you think?" Henry asks. "We can make some changes, of course. I've been living here alone."

"It's . . . fine," Laura says, then sits on one of the chairs, without taking off her coat. The cabin is cold and Henry starts a fire. There's wood stacked outside the door, high as the cabin itself.

"We'd best see to dinner," he says. "I'll get the supplies in. The stove will be hot enough soon."

Laura nods without getting up. She listens to Henry's feet treading the snow to where the mules are hitched. She feels suddenly alone and thinks of the past sixteen days, of the packers, the stories, the laughter. The snow filled the hollows made by their footsteps as they walked. A constant erasing of the past. It is as if none of it happened.

She sighs, then turns to the stove, to the round opening where flames wind around logs like gossamer threads, dangerous, burning. She undoes the top button of her coat and takes a deep breath. Henry will be back soon with the supplies. She removes her bonnet and scarf and pats her hair.

"Laura, I'd like you to meet my partner, Jake."

She steps towards the door where he stands, and he comes forward and shakes her hand. "I'm very pleased to make your acquaintance," he says.

She smiles. "And I too." His handshake is firm, his eyes kind.

"I expect you're tired after your journey. Could I offer you some —"

"You could help me bring in the supplies," Henry says, "so Laura can start cooking while I take the mules back." He pushes the door open, then turns to Jake. "No trouble setting an extra place for you, if you want to have supper with us."

Jake stares at Laura for a moment, as if he were trying to assess her, she thinks. She turns away towards the stove.

"Thanks anyway," Jake says. "We have supper almost ready."

She hears the door shut. *We*, Jake said. He knows that she knows. Her cheeks feel hot. What could she have done? She can't go against Henry's wishes, not in his house. She sits in a chair by the window and stares upwards. *Dear God*, she whispers. *Dear God*. But she can find no other words, no requests for Him. None of her prayers have been answered. She sighs, guilty. Perhaps she's expecting too much. Selfishness is a sin. She begins to pray silently, asking God to forgive her thoughts.

By the time Henry returns from Richfield, Laura has a meal cooking on the stove.

"I see you got water," he says.

"Jake brought it."

He looks at her for a moment. "You didn't go over and —"

"He came to ask if I needed anything. And I did need water."

"You'll have to learn to do things yourself," Henry says. "It's the only way you survive in this country. We're not in England now. Women here do their share of work."

Laura doesn't answer; serves their meal in silence.

"I'll need a few things," she says when they are seated. "Cooking utensils, material for curtains, some odds and ends."

"You make up a list. I'll go on up to Richfield tomorrow. We'll need a bigger bed too."

After supper, Henry shows her where to get water. She brings back a bucketful, heats it in two large pots on the stove, then washes the dishes.

Her trunk lies in the middle of the room. She unpacks her clothes and hangs them on nails which Henry has pounded into the partition between the two rooms. She pushes her empty trunk against the foot of the bed, then stands back to look. It'll do. It's not a very pretty sight, but it'll do. She longs suddenly for a hot bath, a soft chair to curl into, a book to read. Instead, she sits by the stove, staring at the flames until Henry says, "For tonight, I'll sleep by the fire. You take the cot."

He remains seated while she undresses behind the partition and gets into bed. Then, he blows out the lamp. She can see him hunched in the chair, staring into the fire, and she wonders what he's thinking. He's not drinking tonight, although she saw him store the bottles of whiskey under one of the floor planks earlier.

She watches him stir from the chair, then put more wood in the stove. He comes towards her in the darkness, reaches for two blankets she folded and put on the dresser earlier, then returns to lie in front of the fire.

She lies on her side and watches the rise and fall of his chest under the blankets. Tonight, she needs to feel him close to her, to know she's not alone in this wilderness.

"Henry?" she whispers.

"Go to sleep. We'll be up early tomorrow. There's so much to be done."

For a long time she lies listening to his breathing, then finally falls asleep.

For the first few days, Henry helps Laura fix the cabin. Then, by the end of the week, he's drinking again, settled into a routine. He gets up late, goes to Richfield in early afternoon, and returns well past midnight.

At first, Laura is perplexed — what is she doing wrong? She tries to reach Henry with gestures — sits at his feet, caresses his arm — but the gentler she is, the more he rebuffs her.

In the cabin, for two weeks now, she's been alone every evening. Why doesn't Henry come back? She needs someone to talk to. She has grown up among women, has taken for granted shared secrets, closeness, affection. Living with a man is a very different thing. There's a barrier between her and

Henry that doesn't allow for intimacy.

She begins to pace in the small room, feeling the walls closing in. If only she hadn't left England. Her heart begins to pound, harder and harder, until she thinks it will come out of her body.

She runs, sobbing, out of the cabin, into the snow without her coat and beats on Jake's door until the young Indian woman opens it. They stare at each other for a moment.

"I'm afraid," Laura whispers, and holds out her hand.

Without hesitation the Indian woman pulls her into an embrace and lets Laura cry against her shoulder, murmuring, "It's not so bad. Nothing's so bad."

When her sobs turn into hoarse rasps which ache all the way down her windpipe, the Indian woman pushes her gently into a chair and pours her a glass of water.

"I'm Sadie," she says.

✧

Wells, December 17.

Vancouver has almost ceased to exist.

Bridgit took me to Barkerville today. There is much snow on the ground, although it's been clear, sunny, and cold since I arrived. We drove to the parking lot at one end of Barkerville, then put on the cross-country skis and slowly, because it's my first time, made our way up the long narrow street. On either side, there are wooden buildings — houses, hotels, stores, and, at one end, an Anglican Church. Barkerville is slowly being restored, Bridgit told me. Everything rebuilt, recreated, just as it was in the days I write about.

We stopped and looked through the windows of some of the houses.

They are filled with period furniture and wax figures of some of the people who lived here. I found a cabin that I imagine Laura might have lived in.

About half way up the narrow street, the large houses gave way to smaller cabins. "This is the Chinese quarter," Bridgit said, pointing to the writing above the doorways. I looked inside one of the stores. Spices and dry goods filled glass containers on shelves behind a tall counter; delicate Chinese ornaments, plates, cups, spoons, vases, and other porcelain items were carefully displayed under glass and on benches around the store. Bridgit told me that it was all authentic — all found buried.

The Barkerville we saw is built some eighteen feet above the original one. Bridgit said when they dig down, they find corner posts and chimneys. Mining shafts were tunneled beneath the town and often caved in. It was not unusual for a building to sink several feet a year.

We continued for about a mile up a trail after the buildings ended, following what looked like a frozen creek. "This was Richfield," Bridgit said, pointing to the hillside and the creek. "But there were no trees then. The forest was cut back to the top of the hill. It was very desolate and ugly, with mounds of stones and earth everywhere, and most men living in tents."

I looked carefully around me, searching for the spot where Henry and Jake could have built the two cabins. It was difficult to visualize this lush forest barren. Perhaps most disquieting was the unearthly silence, and often I asked Bridgit to stand very still while I tried to hear something, anything. It was as if we were the only two living things.

❖

"So," Henry says. "First thing you did was what I told you not to do."

"She's a fine woman, Henry."

"She's no woman. She's a squaw. Belongs in a whorehouse with the rest of them. People have been known to shoot Indians around here for less than that."

Laura busies herself measuring out grain into a pot. She doesn't like the way Henry is talking. She knows little about him, she realizes. On the trip, their conversations revolved mostly around the landscape, the stopping houses, the people they met. They spoke about their past — safe, in that it was set in the familiarity of England. She's learned very little about his character, Laura thinks now. She has seen him be both gentle and rough, but these are common human traits. She wonders whether he has a bad temper. Is he stubborn? Does he like children? And, what does he expect of a wife, of her?

"Did you hear what I said?" Henry grabs her arm.

She shakes his hand loose. "Henry, you don't even know her. You're judging her because she's Indian. Well, to me she's a woman and I intend to make her my friend."

She thinks for a moment he is going to strike her, and she moves back a step instinctively. He looks away from her suddenly then, and slumps into the chair.

"Already Jake's getting his way," he mumbles.

"Jake has nothing to do with this. He wasn't even there. I went on my own."

"Sure. Well. It's still Jake's fault."

Henry has fallen asleep in a chair. Laura goes to the window and stares out. Henry told her there will be snow until at least May or June, although the creek will thaw before then. Seven months, she thinks, before she can plant a garden. She's certain root vegetables will grow. Potatoes, beets, and turnips. Perhaps she can seed lettuce in pots inside, by the window. She'll ask

Henry to build her a shelf.

Sadie comes out of her cabin and scrambles up one of the banks. Laura watches her until she disappears over the top of the hill. They haven't spoken much, she and Sadie, at least not with words. But Laura feels better in the knowledge that there's a woman nearby — someone who might understand her feelings.

She sighs. Seven months. What is she to do with her time? Back home, she was busy. Reading, teaching the small children. Back home she was useful. Perhaps, when the men return in the spring, there'll be more for her to do.

Laura has questions she wants to ask Sadie. She follows her up the hill one afternoon, a week after her arrival on the creek. She makes a great deal of noise as she walks, hoping that Sadie will stop and wait for her. But Sadie neither turns nor acknowledges her presence. Laura isn't sure whether she does this because Henry is watching (she is aware of it too), or because she wants to be alone. She'll follow, she decides, until Sadie tells her not to.

She thinks about the past month. Already she feels trapped in a monotonous routine. Is this all she can expect of marriage? She cooks meals and waits. Nights when he's home, Henry drinks in front of the fire while she lies in bed. Sometimes, he falls asleep there. Other times, he gropes — no, he attacks her, she thinks. She's learning to disassociate herself mentally. She has stopped praying. There's no comfort in a god who does not listen. She thinks, instead, about Sadie.

Laura scrambles up the top of the hill. It's been a steep climb and she is breathless. Throughout the last part, she's been staring at the ground in front of her, trying to find handholds. She looks up now and gasps at the thick forest that begins less than twenty metres ahead. Sadie sits on a fallen log at the edge, watching her.

"I thought I'd never see another tree," Laura says, brushing snow off the log and sitting next to Sadie.

Sadie smiles.

"Do you know when I arrived from England — it seems so long ago — I couldn't bear the trees, how tall and dark they are. I wanted everything flat and open. Then we came here and suddenly all this open space looked ugly." She laughs. "It's strange, isn't it? How we can look at the same thing and see something different."

"That something different is inside of you," Sadie says.

"Yes. I suppose it is." Laura stretches her legs out in front of her. The toes of her shoes catch the edge of sunlight. Behind her, the forest is already in shadow. "Why do you come up here?" she asks.

"To hear the forest."

"It's deathly quiet."

"When I was little, my brother would take me to the woods to listen to the spirits talk in the voice of the trees and the birds and the deer and the frog."

Laura smiles. One of the packers told her about the Indian spirits who transform themselves into animals, birds, humans, mythical creatures — all revered, some feared. "How could these spirits talk?" she asks.

"They are like your God," Sadie says. "And are mightier than men."

"Well, I don't know about your spirits, but I don't think my God can do very much. At least, he hasn't been listening to me." She pauses. "How old are you, Sadie?"

Sadie shrugs. "Twenty. Maybe more."

"Where is your family?"

"On the coast, maybe. May be dead. I been gone five years. Since I become Jake's woman."

"You've been together that long?" Laura thinks Henry said Sadie was a recent development.

Sadie nods. "All except maybe one year. That was right after

". . . I mean, before Jake first came up here." She pauses. "You ask too many questions. You don't hear if you talk all the time."

"Will you tell me about the spirits?" Laura asks.

"Maybe. Some time. Not now."

Laura nods, but Sadie has already turned her head away and now faces forward, eyes closed. Laura gets up from the log and walks towards the edge of the hill. The sun has set so quickly that she hasn't noticed until now, when she suddenly feels cool. Before going down the hill, she turns and looks back at the log. Sadie is sitting in the same position, so still and small that if Laura did not know she was there, she would have mistaken her for one of the forest's shadows.

✧

March, 1986.

Perhaps there is no loneliness worse than that which exists when two people live apart under the same roof. Marc and I have been doing this for months. Why does it take so long to leave? I've written him a poem. If only it were so easy.

✧

11. *The Long Withdrawal*

SUMMER

On the longest day of the year
the Yukon night is a brush stroke
lightning dusk
when the sun dips into a palette of mountains
then emerges dripping crimson
on the crests of the river
we have become

confluent now
we flow the stream
elusive
do you recall the merge —
distant peaks
tenuous trails
and how we were hurled together
in the mouth of rapids?

   (the stiletto
   sinks silent/violent
   between ribs)

Now we are calm, distilled
the churn of sediment
so settled in our marriage bed
we don't see the sandbar up ahead.

Hush, don't speak
words are too wet
and gravel sticks too easy

let silence lick us separate streams
Hurry past

  (retraction
  springs internal bleeding)
We converge in a whirlpool
shivering in the flat of a raven's shadow
arms clasp a cold embrace
silt grinds
between breaths.

AUTUMN

Mountains devour the sun
recede the Yukon day to dusk
the wind insists, erratic
we shirk, skirt.

  (Denial, a dam
  fragile as muslin
  porous as clay)

Come, kindle a fire
in the river's bowels
we could thaw bedded rock
with our hands
melt lava
with our mouths.

  (ache coagulates
  massive/impassive)

The river dwindles
to the thin of a pencil
we search new tributaries
strangled/triangled
slash deep welts
side by side.

WINTER

An Arctic frost moves in
the river yields to the wind
lies still
legs rigid to the shore
between thighs
a pulsing stream
you or I oceanbound?

We have become so fixed and fluid
we need not speak
listen
beneath the ice
love snaps a whip
and memories —
eager huskies with marble eyes —
tug the harness
some die
in swift explosions
some linger
scraping the underside
but we are deaf and numb
in the rigors of frost.

SPRING

Night froths
we are bundled on separate edges
of a river bed
drinking the melt of shores by day

we can no longer taste each other
tongues thick with hoar

the river curses in a swell
uproarious

we can no longer shout
across the din
throats hoarse with torpor

   (dying of exposure
   bodies riddled/needled)

the sun spits out more day
a lukewarm surface thaw
we languish in the river's fingers
frostbitten
listen to the break up
in a nearby bed
taste the promise of salt
in river mouths.

Come closer
listen.

Henry

Henry's back to digging during the day. He and Jake have decided to work through the winter. All of last season, they sank a shaft, a crude wooden structure.

They've taken out small amounts of gold, enough to encourage them. Henry is convinced that if they dig down to bedrock, they'll strike a vein.

He enjoys the hard physical labor. It tires and leaves him with less time to think about Laura and him. He senses that she's not happy, and he feels guilty. He buys whatever she asks for; there is food in their cabin; and he doesn't expect her to work. What more can he do? Sometimes, Laura sits by the window and stares at the snow for hours. He doesn't want to know what she's thinking. Not really. He was very uncomfortable on both occasions when Laura tried to talk to him about personal things. Like last Sunday, when they were walking back from Richfield after Mass, and she asked him if he believed in God. Or the time she wanted to know how and where he met Jake. He doesn't feel right talking about his father's death or about his feelings. Those are not things to share with a woman, he thinks, unless she's your mother. And Laura is his wife.

He and Jake work all day and cover the shaft with boards at night, to keep the snow out. Henry dreads the evenings, irritated by Laura's silences. Sometimes he talks to her about the claim or tells her a miner's story he remembers, but she says little in response. He doesn't think she's very interested. Perhaps it was a mistake to marry her, to bring her up here. He hadn't thought about what she'd do once she was here. His mother had busied herself with knitting and sewing and caring for him. He'd never questioned whether she was happy. She was a woman and she did women's things. Why couldn't Laura be like her?

They haven't talked about Sadie again, not once in the past two months. But Henry knows the two women are spending a lot of time together. In the afternoons. He wonders what they do over the top of the hill. One day he'll sneak up and see for himself. For now, he's almost glad Laura spends time with Sadie. It lessens his responsibility towards her. In the evenings, he often visits some of the men on the other claims, and drinks till dawn.

He was foolish to think that marriage would change everything; that a wife would take over his life and manage it better than he could. Instead, he feels increasingly isolated.

Sometimes, when he watches Laura bent over the stove, he wants to reach out and touch her. It would be so easy to love her. But he is afraid. Love drives people away — his mother, his father, Jake — leaves him vulnerable.

He drains himself of feeling by working feverishly, filling the bucket with shovel after shovel of gravel, until his arms ache and Jake makes him stop.

12. *Personal Account by A. Jordan*

". . . We'd been digging a shaft all summer, down to seventy feet. Doing it all by the bucketful too. Thing that kept us going was we were convinced we'd hit bedrock sooner or later. Other claims had dug down that deep and found more gold than they knew what to do with. But it wasn't like a guarantee or anything. You could sink two shafts side by side and only one would yield anything. Still, we kept digging and planning what we'd do with the gold once we found it. Most people talked about leaving the goldfields, maybe going out east or south. But few ever hit it rich enough to actually do it. In all my years up there, I never made more than enough to get me through the winter . . . ."

"What do you think you'll do with the money?" Laura asks Henry. "I mean, if you find the gold."

When they quit digging today, they had reached a stiff blue clay which Henry is certain lies on bedrock. He shrugs. "You can do whatever you want once you got money."

"Yes, but what will you do?" She stares and he turns away.

"Hadn't thought about it."

She's pushing her fork around her plate, dividing the food into small piles. It irritates Henry.

"Why don't you eat?" he says. "You must be hungry." He empties his whiskey glass in two gulps.

"Sadie says that she and Jake are going to build a hotel," Laura announces. "With nice rooms and private baths. There's nothing like that here now."

"I don't much care what Sadie says." Henry refills his glass. "Besides, I already knew about the hotel. Jake told me."

But this is not true. Jake doesn't tell him anything any more. Of course, Henry reasons, it's only because one of them is in the shaft and the other above. If they were working side by side, Jake would have told him. "I don't know what you find to talk about with that woman," he says.

Laura shrugged. "Sadie? Oh . . . things . . . you know?"

"No, I don't know. What things?"

"About living here and the Indian ways —"

"Why should you care about Indian ways? You're not one of them."

"I'm . . . interested." She stares at her food.

He wants to say something nasty about Sadie, about the hotel, about Jake, about how the three of them plan things without telling him. He shakes his head instead, and downs his drink.

He isn't interested in their things anyway. And he won't tell them his plans of buying a new claim and expensive equipment; of hiring men and having the biggest operation on the creek. No, he won't tell them.

After dinner, he knocks on Jake's door. "You want to work through the night?"

Henry goes down the shaft this time. Little by little he works out the blue clay but, as he lifts each bit, water spurts in its place.

Henry curses. "Get that pump working harder," he shouts up the shaft, his voice hollow. Jake can't hear him. He gives three tugs on the rope. His feet are beginning to stick to the wet clay. Each step makes a loud, smacking sound which reverberates all the way up the shaft. He curses again. No change in the pump. He supposes it's working to capacity, though it can barely keep up with the water. Finally, he comes to the last piece of clay — a section about two-feet square. He digs and pulls and lifts until it begins to move. "Last piece," he shouts to himself. "Last son-of-a-bitch to go." He chops the piece in half with his shovel so he can lift it into the bucket. But, when he removes the first bit, water gushes from beneath, as if he's uncovered a spring. At first, he tries to cover the space with his feet, stamping on it as one would to put out a fire. But the water continues to spring, quickly covering his boots and ankles. Henry curses again and again. The water level is rising rapidly. At this rate, he'll soon drown. He'll have to empty the bucket so he can get into it himself. He prays that Jake will wait for his signal before pulling up the rope. He'll surely notice the shift in weight — bucket filled and emptied — and probably will be wondering what's happening below.

By the time the bucket is empty enough for Henry to step into it, the water reaches half way up his thighs. He grabs hold of the side of the bucket and gives the rope a yank. The bucket, too, is filled with water. He'll have to help get it up before he can jump in. He tugs and strains. The bucket begins to rise. Henry grabs the rope just as it starts to move out of his reach and jumps for the side of the bucket. The lurch makes Jake stop above. Henry breathes a great sigh and hauls himself in. Then, he yanks the rope once more and the bucket slowly begins to rise.

Henry shudders as he goes up the dark tunnel. The lantern is hooked to the top of the bucket, illuminating a small bit of the shaft above him. Months of work are represented in the walls. They've dug out each bit with their shovels, just the two of them. And now this. Finally, he feels the cool night air and sees Jake's face above him, questioning.

"Water. Filling up so fast, I didn't know if I'd get out in time." He jumps out of the bucket, then the two of them lower the lantern as far as they can reach, and look below. Soon, they can see the water rising up the shaft, silently and quickly until it reaches them, icy and fresh. "We've built a goddamn well," Henry says, shivering. His clothes are soaked. "Let's get the pump going again. We'll beat this."

But Jake shakes his head. "Ain't no use. We're not going to get that water out no matter how many pumps we use. I've seen this kind of thing before. You said it right the first time. We got ourselves a goddamn well." He picks up the lantern and takes Henry's arm. "Come on. You're going to freeze solid unless we get those clothes off you."

In the morning, Henry sits quiet at the kitchen table while Laura serves breakfast. He's only had three hours sleep and his head aches. Jake joins them for coffee. Henry sits glum, listening to the sound of his spoon hitting the side of his mug.

"So what are we going to do now?" Laura asks. She looks pale and tired, Henry thinks.

"I got a little money saved up," Jake says. "I was thinking now might be a good time to buy into the Cameron claim."

"What? And abandon this one? After all the work we've put

into it?" Henry shifts in his chair. He can't believe Jake would even suggest this. "We'll pump it out," he says. "There's gold under all that water."

"Might be, but we'll never see it. Look," Jake says. "I've got enough saved up to get us each a share. They've got lots of equipment and men over there. We stand a much better chance pooling in with them."

Henry stares into his cup. Jake, always with the answers and the money. He can't accept the offer, he has too much pride for that. "You want to throw away all our work, fine. But I'm staying here and pumping this one out."

Laura touches his arm. "Henry, you can't work the shaft by yourself. And Jake knows more about these things. He's been mining a lot longer than you have."

He shakes her hand off. "And you know nothing about these things. So keep quiet."

She withdraws her hand and rests it on her lap. He feels sorry immediately and wishes he could take back the words.

"If you don't want to take my offer," Jake says, "you could still go over and hire on to work. They're paying ten dollars a day. That's not bad wages."

Henry stiffens. "You do what you want, Jake. I'm sticking it out here. I'll get another partner." He pushes his chair away from the table, grabs his coat from the hook, and goes outside.

Jake buys into the Cameron claim as planned, while Henry spends most days pumping water. After a while, he quits doing even this and just sits beside the shaft, watching the widening circles made by the pebbles he throws into the deep water. Laura keeps trying to persuade him to go and join Jake. They have bitter quarrels which leave Henry feeling sorry afterwards, but he refuses to give in.

The Cameron claim strikes coarse gold. Jake owns one sixth. Henry, on hearing the news, dons snowshoes and his pack and goes to Antler where he holes up in a hotel, and remains drunk for six days.

Jake comes to get him on the seventh, and Henry wonders if Laura has sent him.

"Come on, Henry. Time to go home." Jake pulls his legs over the side of the bed.

"Leave me alone. All of you. Just leave me alone." He cups his head in his hands.

"I've got enough money for both of us. Let me give you some, just as a loan, until you get on your feet."

"Stop trying to help me," Henry shouts. "I'm sick of it. I'll make it on my own." He's had bad luck, that's all. Ever since he arrived here, one bad thing after another.

"You'll do fine," Jake says. "Come on. Let's get you cleaned up."

Although only superficially, he and Jake resume their friendship — begin talking again. Henry goes to work at the Cameron claim for wages. He and Laura hardly speak now. He wants to apologize for everything, but he can't. He avoids her as much as possible.

One of the miners' wives dies during the winter. Her husband is anxious to take her body to Victoria for embalming before the temperature warms up. There are no undertakers here, and the body has been placed in a tin-and-wooden coffin made by the men, and stored in a cabin at the back of Richfield. The miner offers twelve dollars a day and two thousand dollars to any man who will make the journey to Victoria with him. On hearing this, Henry decides that he will volunteer for the job. It's his plan to look for work elsewhere, perhaps even in Victoria. There's nothing to keep him here any longer. Even Laura doesn't need him, she has Sadie and Jake. Let them look after her.

He keeps his plan secret and goes to see the miner to make

the arrangements. The two thousand dollars are to go to Laura, along with a note in which he explains where he's going and that he'll be back for her as soon as he has prospects of work. He doesn't know why he writes this, because he doesn't intend to return, ever. Early that January, on the pretext of going to Antler, Henry leaves the cabin for Victoria.

❖

June, 1986.

I let Marc read Laura and Henry's story so far.
"Is it true?" *he asked, always concerned with details.*
"Literally or metaphorically?"
"Literally. Can you substantiate any of this story?"
"Not necessarily."
"Then what's the point? You can't invent history. Even family history."
How to explain my need for context?
"Imagine," *I told him,* "the photograph of a woman barefoot in sand. Who is she? Where is she?"
He watched me, suspicious. "How old is she?"
"My age."
"What's she wearing?"
"Shirt and pants."
"Is she smiling?"
"No."
"She's a young woman at a seaside resort — not having a very good time."
"Imagine the same photograph," *I told him,* "taken from a different perspective. An aerial view. A desert. Dunes combed to the horizon. The woman is alone."

Laura

January 1863. "It's my fault he left," Laura says to Sadie the day after Jake brings her Henry's note along with the money. "I don't think I was a very good wife." The two of them are in Sadie's cabin. It's much brighter than hers; Jake has made a ledge half-way up the wall and whitewashed the top part. On the ledge are miniature clay figures of birds, animals, and mythical creatures Sadie insists are real. Laura loves to watch Sadie make these while they sit together.

"Don't go blaming yourself," Sadie says. "There's a lot you don't know about Henry. May be even Henry doesn't know himself very well."

Laura sighs. "Who does? Here I am, barely seventeen, married and separated. What am I to do?"

Sadie smiles. "You'll be all right. You will find power inside you."

"Oh Sadie, I wish I really believed in your spirits and their power. I could use some of it now." She pauses. "I did try to be a good wife to Henry. But I couldn't . . . you know . . . get close to him. I would have liked to talk to him like we talk." She leans forward. "Do you think all men are like this?"

Sadie laughs and pats her arm. "I don't think you can say all men are the same. Or all women are the same."

In Henry's opinion, all Indians are the same. Laura nods. "I just don't know much about men."

"Don't judge them all by one."

"You don't like Henry any better than he likes you, do you?"

Sadie stares into her mug of coffee. "I feel sorry for him. But you're right. I don't like him much."

Sadie reaches into the water bucket beside her and takes out a piece of clay wrapped in cloth. Laura watches her peel the fabric away slowly, waiting for her to continue.

"He's caused Jake nothing but worry since he arrived." Sadie breaks off a small piece of the blue clay and begins to work it in her fingers.

"But Henry told me it was Jake's idea to form a partnership."

"Jake felt responsible for Henry," Sadie says. "Not that he should have." She sets the clay down and leans back in her chair, sighing. "Jake and me were together three years until he went back to San Francisco. Had some business to take care of, so he left me up the island coast with my family. Then he and Stew — that was Henry's father — they came back together from San Francisco. As soon as they arrived in Victoria, Jake left Stew in a tent — Stew didn't have much money to spend on a hotel — and came up island to get me." Sadie pauses and sighs again. "When we got back, we found Stew in the tent. Shot. He'd been dead three, four days. We buried him, Jake and me. Then Jake went to meet Henry. Jake thought if he'd been there, it wouldn't have happened." Sadie picks up the clay and squeezes it between her hands.

"What did you do?" Laura asks.

"Went back to my family and waited. Jake thought he should be looking after Henry right then. He said he'd send for me soon as he was settled. So I came up the year before you. Jake arranged it with some of the packers going up."

"Poor Henry." Now that he's gone, Laura can think of him differently. He wasn't much older when he arrived than she was. "To have lost his mother and father so close together . . . it must have been very difficult for Henry." She hardly remembers her own parents. At the orphanage, she learned to like her own company. Some of the girls were like sisters to her, but they all knew the time would come when they would separate. Laura was prepared; she accepted the impermanence of her situation. One day, she would have a family and things would be different. "What am I going to do, Sadie?" she says.

"Nothing is as I thought it would be."

"There's not much you can do until spring. You've got money and a house to live in. Even if you decide to go back to England or Victoria, you have to wait until the road opens. It's probably better this way. It'll give you a chance to think it out. May be Henry will send for you like he says in the note."

"I don't think so. If he'd meant to, he'd have talked to me abut it. He ran off."

"At least he left you some money."

"It won't last forever." Laura stretches. "But it will do until I figure out something."

"The snow will melt," Sadie says.

Mid-morning on April 14th, Jake bursts into Laura's cabin without knocking.

"It's Sadie," he whispers.

"What's happened to Sadie?" Laura pushes past him outside towards the cabin.

"Don't go in there." Jake holds her arm.

She turns. His face is red and wet with tears. "What's happened?"

"Sadie's dead."

"Sadie dead? But I just saw her last evening. She wasn't ill. It can't be."

"She's been murdered. Oh —"

Laura struggles to swallow the lump beginning to form in her throat. "But who . . . why would anyone . . ."

"I don't know. I just found her." Jake's voice breaks and he begins to weep aloud. Laura embraces him and they both cling tightly to each other for comfort. Then, when Laura pulls him towards the cabin, he follows without objection.

Sadie lies on the bed, eyes closed. Laura might think her asleep were it not for the dark coagulated blood covering her abdomen and hands. "Oh my God," Laura whispers. She runs outside and vomits.

Jake follows her, holds her a moment. "There's no need for you to come back in," he says. "I'll take care of her."

"No!" Laura breathes deeply. She must regain control. "You see to the sheriff or whatever must be done. I'll take care of Sadie. I'll be all right."

"Laura, you don't have to . . ."

"She was my friend too. I want to do what's right. You go for the sheriff." She swallows twice before re-entering the cabin. At the doorway, she stops. "Jake?"

"What is it?"

"It's got to be done in the Indian way. You can't bury her like a white woman. She wouldn't want that."

Jake hesitates. "I don't know how to go about it."

"I know someone who does," Laura says.

✧

Vancouver, January 3.

What am I doing here? What am I doing? What am I? The passing of time. Passing time. Passing judgement too. On everything. Everyone. Time. I write it in these pages, then discard each paper — a neat pile, numbered. It is like plucking petals off a daisy — he loves me, he loves me not . . . What will remain when all the writing stops? Don't think about it. Don't think. Don't.

Go one. Continue. You are in control. You are me. I am in control. Amusing myself. Aren't I? Passing time. History. Make-believe. Henry and Laura are making themselves up. As we all do. Who will write me down to the stem?

Don't. Don't.

I can only surmise what might have happened in the months between

January and April — between Henry's departure and Sadie's murder. I am, however, certain that Henry was the murderer, although it was never proven, nor was there any evidence to suggest that he had returned to the goldfields. The presence of a new character, Tetlaneetsa (Sadie's brother), one about whom I found no mention until Sadie's death, has led me to make certain assumptions.

⋄

February or March 1863. A flashback.

One evening, Laura is sitting by the fire, reading a book Jake has brought from Antler when she suddenly feels she's being watched. She looks up at the window. Two eyes stare back, although she can't make out the outline of a face. There appears to be no hair, no nose, no mouth, just two eyes hanging in the middle of the darkness. Laura screams and covers her face. When she looks up again, the eyes are gone. She begins to cry, wondering if she's going mad; if the cold and loneliness have finally become too much. She thought she was coping. Isn't she? She scrambles into bed fully clothed and pulls the blankets over her head.

A knock. Laura covers her ears. Then Sadie's voice, "Laura? It's me. Sadie. Open the door. I know you're awake."

Laura sighs, gets up and unbolts the door.

"You must have had a fright," Sadie says, then laughs. "Tetlaneetsa — my brother — told me. He was looking for me and came to the wrong cabin."

"What's he doing skulking around here in the middle of the night? I almost died of fright." Laura, relieved, embarrassed, and a little disappointed to discover that her presumed madness can be so easily explained.

"It's not the middle of the night. Don't exaggerate. He meant no harm." Sadie, always practical.

"What's he doing here anyway?" Laura says, irritated.

"Come with news of my family. To see how I am." Sadie pauses. "Tetlaneetsa thinks I should not be living with a white man. He says I have forgotten the teachings of my people. But I have not. He would like to take me home."

"Would you go?"

"No. But it will not stop him from trying to convince me."

The next morning, Laura rises at dawn and sees the sky has cleared. Long thick icicles hang from the edge of the cabin roof and sink into the snow that reaches almost to the window. She imagines herself an icy princess in a fairytale castle slatted with glistening crystal beads. Those long hard fingers can seal her inside, freeze her into the loneliness of the cabin. She shivers and waits until the sun rises over the mountain, then puts on a pair of Henry's pants, coat, and boots and trudges through the snow up the hill. She walks into the forest, following the contour of the hill towards Barkerville, trying to empty her mind, to listen, as Sadie has shown her.

She walks a little over a mile, her head down, watching the ground when, suddenly, she steps out of the shadows. She stops and looks up. She is two feet into a small clearing which, to her right, extends over the edge of the hill. She hesitates, trying to decide if beneath the snow there might be some hidden danger — water perhaps, a pool draining into the center of the earth. She shakes her head — she's being silly — and steps gingerly across the clearing. The snow is hard enough to support her weight, and she sinks only two or three inches, her boots making crunching pleasant sounds. She stops in the middle and turns her face to the sun. She will come here in summer. There will be grass and wildflowers. If she raises herself on tiptoe, she can see the settlement of Barkerville below. Jake and Sadie will build a hotel there. She can watch them from here.

A small gust of wind blows her hair away from her forehead. Laura stiffens. Smoke. She turns, startled, and sees for the first time a small fire burning at the opposite edge of the clearing. She shivers. At first she cannot see anyone, then as she continues to stare at the fire, she sees an Indian man sitting motionless to one side of it. His body is wrapped in a blanket made of bark so that only his face shows. He's watching her — the same eyes she saw the night before.

"Oh," she exclaims. "You've frightened me again."

He does not move.

"I'm Sadie's friend," she says, then thinks this stupid. "You're Sadie's brother."

He watches her motionless. She could be invisible, she thinks, he does not acknowledge her in any way. Confused, she says, "I'm sorry. I didn't mean to intrude," thinking suddenly that he is performing some Indian rite; trying to remember the things Sadie told her about. She turns and walks quickly back the way she came.

Once in the woods, she admonishes herself. She shouldn't have said anything. What if he isn't Sadie's brother? Of course he is. She wouldn't forget those eyes. By the time she reaches the cabin, she has decided Sadie's brother is very rude and it doesn't matter one bit one way or another. He'll be gone soon and the clearing will be hers.

The rest of the day, the whole next day, Laura wills herself not to go up the hill. The third morning, she can't stop herself.

"Where are you going?" Sadie's voice.

"Nowhere." Her own voice too breathless.

"Of course you are."

"Walking. I feel like a prisoner in that cabin."

"Wait. I'll go with you."

She can't say no. There's no reason to say no. Is there?

They walk in the opposite direction to the clearing. Laura is not very talkative. She listens. Sadie says her brother has gone back home. When they return and can see the cabins from the top of the hill, Laura says, "I'll walk on a little. I don't want to go back yet."

Sadie shrugs and leaves her.

Laura walks slowly, following her own tracks made two days earlier. There has been no snow to erase them. This time she smells the smoke before she enters the clearing. *He is still there.* She makes herself take small even steps. He sits to one side of the fire and watches her approach. She notices a shelter made of branches. Was it there the other day?

"Hello again," she says in a small voice, embarrassed, then finds a stump nearby and sits down also.

He doesn't speak. At least not this time. Perhaps not for days. She returns each afternoon, irresistibly drawn by something, no, someone so alien. Several nights, she thinks she sees his face in her window. But she can't be sure. She could be in the midst of a fantasy.

Vancouver, January 15.

Who knows what may have happened in that clearing. Perhaps the coupling of two solitary creatures; perhaps only the wary stalking of the observed and the observer. Hunted and hunter. But who was who? I can't decide. But I'm sure Henry followed Laura one day and found them together. He left no trace of his being there, other than Sadie's blood.

Laura washes Sadie's body and lays her on the cot under a clean sheet and blankets, although there is no need for this precaution. She leaves when Jake returns with the sheriff, and walks quickly up to the clearing. Tetlaneetsa will know what to do.

Wood is stacked neatly beside the shelter but there is no fire. Laura touches the cold ashes, searches, and calls his name — sounding awkward to her own ears. Does he know already? She sits and waits a while, then goes home.

Jake is alone. Sadie's body has been taken away to be stored until the thaw or until he can decide where to bury her.

"I told the sheriff her brother had been around. He never liked me, you know. Sheriff thinks he may have done this."

"You can't think Tetlaneetsa would murder his own sister!"

Jake looks at her, frowning, and Laura turns her head away. She can't tell him. She can tell no one.

"You don't know him. He tried to take her away from here." But Jake's voice sounds unconvinced. "Anyway, who else would have done this? There was no reason." He covers his face with his hands and begins to sob.

Laura stands uncertain for a moment. She too wants to cry but feels that Jake needs her strength right now. She holds him against her shoulder and caresses his head, feeling irrevocably alone.

Vancouver, January 16.

Listen. There is an echo called David. This echo tastes of summer sun and forest fires; this echo rolls off the tip of the tongue in salted droplets; this echo swells in afterwaves. Don't listen. Don't.

I have stopped my morning vomiting.

August 1863. Laura and Jake have just opened the Caller Hotel. Her two thousand dollars make her one-fourth owner. She has stayed in the Cariboo because Jake needs her; Sadie forms a link between them; she has nowhere to go. Tetlaneetsa. What if he comes back? At first, she returned often to the clearing, hoping to see him. But all that remains are the ashes of his last fire.

The hotel is situated in Barkerville — about a mile down the canyon from Richfield. Her clearing is above.

Laura likes Barkerville, the excitement and activity there. Merchants have arrived from the coast in great numbers to service the growing community. The miners have begun to abandon their tents and rough shelters, in favor of wooden houses on log posts in a row near Williams Creek. Boardwalks front all the houses at irregular levels which, though interesting to look at, make walking unsafe. The street itself is crooked, about eighteen feet wide, muddy and rutted. But despite all these drawbacks, unlike Richfield and Antler before it, Laura thinks, Barkerville has the appearance of a permanent town.

They have told everyone she is a widow, and she has reverted to her maiden name, Browler. Jake convinced her that this would be the best thing — to keep people from talking and men from harassing her. She is a woman alone in a predominantly male town.

Jake supervised the building of the hotel, and Laura chose fixtures from catalogues, which Jake later bought in Victoria.

On his last trip to Victoria, she begged him to buy a piano — an expense he thought too extravagant. She said to him, "I can play several nights a week; we'll have dances; it'll make all the difference to the hotel's success." Jake laughed and reminded her that there were not enough women on the creek for dances. But in the end, he agreed to buy the piano.

Laura has her own reasons for wanting the piano. She needs something in which to lose herself. She is lonelier than ever, but tries to hide it from Jake. She has stopped going to the clearing — she can almost make herself believe that Tetlaneetsa never existed.

A few days after their opening, Laura receives a letter from Henry, dated July. He says that he's working at road building; that he's befriended someone with a claim along the Fraser River and is thinking of going into partnership with him. Laura shakes her head as she reads. Between the lines, she can sense a desperation in his words. She burns the letter after she's read it to Jake. For a few weeks Laura is anxious, worried that Henry might come back. She is settled now and comfortable with herself and her plans. She doesn't want him ruining everything.

April 1864. Laura has enough money to buy a small house which, although in need of repair, suits her very well. She has windows fitted and a new stove installed. The house has three main rooms — a sitting room, a kitchen-dining room, and a small bedroom in the back. She owns only the house and the surface rights. But so far, no one has claimed the underground rights. She gambled on the fact that the house stands removed from the creek, although she knows that nothing would obstruct a miner pursuing his luck.

Other than with Jake, she has spent no time socializing since her arrival in Barkerville. She has shunned the advances of the miners she meets at the hotel, having decided that if she were to re-marry, it would not be to a miner.

Jake and Laura walk together in the warm summer night. They're settled into a routine. He walks her home after the late dance evenings, and always waits till she is inside before returning to the hotel. Tonight, she feels him hesitant beside her, as if he has something to tell her. She unlocks the door and waits before entering. Jake stands silent for a moment, then he touches her arm.

"It's not natural for someone your age to be alone," he says. "It's cold and lonely here."

Laura tries to see his eyes, there in the darkness, but he is looking down at the wooden slats in front of the door.

"Don't say any more," she whispers. "I can't."

"Not ever?" He looks straight at her then, and she turns away.

"I don't know, Jake. I just don't know."

"Go on inside," he says, pushing her lightly through the doorway. "You'll catch cold."

Inside, she pauses a moment, listening to his footsteps on the stairs. "Jake," she calls softly and he stops. "I — thank you." He nods and touches his hat before continuing on his way.

❖

Vancouver, January 20.

Is the present forged out of the past or is the past sculpted by the present? My pen wavers somewhere in the middle, and the ink begins to dry. Tired, cold, lonely. Some nights I pull the blankets over my head. Some mornings I am surprised by light, rain, tide, clouds; by the earth's vital repetition of routine.

There is no point pretending I really know this story. But some of it, perhaps, is true. I've gathered facts and shaped them. Suddenly, I find myself with too many missing pieces; with no desire to connect them.

Laura and Jake? No. Too easy. Perhaps in a fairy tale.

Laura and Tetlaneetsa? No. It wouldn't have been possible in those days. She never saw him again. Perhaps somewhere near that clearing his bones are bleached dry. Perhaps Henry's hands have dug a grave and buried him. I don't know.

Facts. Time passage. When winter breaks, Williams Creek rises and floods Main Street. Laura still has not overcome her fear of this spring freshet, though she prepares for it each year at this time. She stays indoors, listening to the water rush under the house, certain that at any moment, the supporting pylons will break in two. It reminds her of her trip across the sea — waves crashing against the hull.

The miner's tunnels which extend dangerously close to, and sometimes even beneath the houses, often cave in under the force of the water. Last year, she watched a house sink six feet into the ground. But the slag piles continue to grow on either side of the creek. She wonders if the mining will ever stop; if there will ever be trees on the hillside and meadows with wildflowers. Barkerville is set in a narrow valley between two mountains. When she first came, she felt hemmed in by the dark evergreens and dreamed of open spaces where she could watch the sun rise and set. Now, when she looks to the hillsides, she sees only rocks and gravel and miners' tents — mounds of grey on grey. In the summer, she often puts on men's trousers and boots and wanders up, past the working men, making her way to the clearing.

It is from here that she watches Fanny Bendixen and her Hurdy Gurdy girls arrive by stagecoach this spring.

13. *Poems by Anne McCrae, 1962*

THE HURDY-GURDY DAMSELS: 1866

White women few those days
though needed for cooking and dancing,
this being before
women had other uses.

The Hurdy-Gurdies, Dutch maidens
from impoverished homes,
bought with slick promises,
bound to service at 50¢ a dance
until a thousand fares are paid
with the thrashing of their bodies
hoisted to rafters,
cotton print skirts and crinolines overturned
in a kaleidoscope of men,
in the turnstile
of soiled hands, black fingernails
and muscles ruddy and starched with dredging
on Williams Creek.

English a foreign language they surmount
in a rote of vulgarisms
spilling from miners' tongues,
set to the rhythm of music without euphony,
set to the clamorous shrieking of fiddles
without harmony.

When they have paid their debt,
some marry miners,
trade one bondage for another.

THE BALLAD OF FANNY BENDIXEN

Chaperone to the Hurdy-Gurdy girls
Fanny Bendixen emerges
as a staunch God-fearing woman
a paradigm of virtue.

Hushed whispers rustle underfoot
lemures of glamours passed
in 'Frisco as the paramour
of a wealthy murderous man.

Mansions, diamonds, silks, furs,
renounced for love
on Williams Creek, women are poor,
coquettish smiles and parted loins
purchase the jingling sound of coins;
the jilted lover pours his voice
in a splash of nitric acid on Fanny's modest gown
in a gush of blood spurting from her fiance's brow.

Undaunted, the San Francisco belle
travels to Williams Creek
and buys the Parlour Hotel.

On June 25th, the Parlour Hotel opens its doors. Laura has agreed to provide the music for the opening night. All of Barkerville comes, including Mrs. Liddy who normally crusades against the evils of alcohol. Laura smiles when she sees Mr. Liddy lead her to a chair in a corner of the room. They are all curious about the German girls: their stout bodies and large feet, their colorful costumes — full printed-cotton skirts with red sashes at the waist and a head-dress like a turban knotted in front. Laura begins the first tune and, amid cheers and shouts, the miners rush for partners. Some of the girls are agile; all are enthusiastic. They are hoisted to and fro, skirts whirling, feet flying. Laura plays lively music and stops every five minutes or so to give all the men a chance at a partner. She knows the procedure; she has heard Fanny explain it to the girls. After each dance, they are to take their partners to the bar where, for a dollar, each will receive a drink — alcohol for the men and a fruit juice for the girls. The next morning, the girls will collect fifty cents on the dollar for each of their customers.

A little past midnight, Laura excuses herself. She's happy, but a little tired from playing since seven o'clock. An old miner runs back to his cabin and returns with a hand-organ. Laura leaves the Parlour Hotel after many handshakes and a quick hug from Fanny. She walks down Main Street in the warm evening air, wearing only a thin muslin dress. Light pours into the narrow street from the windows of the hotels, shops, and houses which front it. It is comforting, familiar. She laughs softly and does a few dance steps of her own. She can't remember the last time she felt so light. She twirls on her toes, holding up one side of her gown in her hand. As she approaches the Liddy house, she thinks she sees the curtains move. Mrs. Liddy left the hotel long before, but Mr. Liddy remained behind. Laura walks very stiffly past the window, then giggles as she runs the rest of the way home. It is at times like these, when she feels flushed and giggly, that she most wishes she had someone.

She sobers as soon as she looks up at her house. She left a lantern burning and, through the window, can see a shadow move across the inner wall of the main room. She stops and her heartbeat quickens. She is not brave enough to climb the stairs alone. She turns and begins to quickly retrace her steps.

"Laura."

She knows the voice.

"I hope I didn't frighten you."

She takes a deep breath and turns. "What on earth are you doing here at this time of night? Of course you frightened me." She walks brusquely past him up the stairs. "Well, come on." She steps inside, goes directly to one of the armchairs and collapses into it, exhausted.

"You don't look too happy to see me," Henry says.

"Well, what did you expect? How long has it been? Two, three years? No word. I might have re-married."

"But we're still married."

"You could have been dead for all I knew." She sighs. "Why have you come?" She doesn't want him here. She doesn't want him to stake a claim on her as he does on those plots of ground. She has worked hard for herself. She watches him from her chair. He appears much older and many lines furrow his brow. She wonders if he ever laughs. "Why have you come?" she repeats when he doesn't answer.

He stands, uncertain, shifting his weight from foot to foot. "You've changed," he says.

"Oh, sit down. You're making me nervous." She closes her eyes and rests her head against the back of the chair. Yes, she supposes, she has changed. She's learned to depend only on herself and has grown strong because of it. She stares up at Henry through half-slitted eyes. He sits on the edge of a chair, fiddling with the hat he holds between his long thin hands. She feels sorry for him suddenly. He looks so vulnerable, child-like. Her tone softens. "Is anything wrong?"

Henry clears his throat. "Not really," he says. "I just thought — well, we could start over, you know — I could work at the hotel with Jake." He sits quiet, waiting for her answer.

"Things have changed," she says flatly.

"Oh, I don't expect . . ." He bites his lip. "Laura, please let me stay. I've got nowhere to go."

She watches him sit, head hung, eyes staring at the brim of the hat he presses between his fingers over and over. She remembers their early days together, the trip to the goldfields. It's not enough.

"You can't stay."

"Is there someone else? Is that it?"

Laura watches him, silent. She does not need to explain anything to him. "Jake and me," she says, then bites her lip. She doesn't know why she said this. Perhaps to anger him; to hurt him a little.

Henry's back stiffens, the vulnerability suddenly gone. Laura is afraid.

"Jake? You and Jake?"

"Henry, please leave." She forces herself to sound calm.

"I don't believe it," he says.

"Believe what you like."

He moves closer; stands over her until her knuckles whiten as she grips the arms of the chair. She keeps her face composed. For a moment, she thinks he will hit her, then he turns and leaves, slamming the door behind him.

She locks herself inside, and only then do her knees start to shake.

✧

Vancouver. January 26.

Almost finished. Yet, I'm not sure any of this explains my confusion. I am unfair to Henry because he is a character I don't understand any more than he understands Laura, or she him. Man and woman. Random magnetic forces which attract and repel. In this constant strife for communion, there is also the inevitable discovery of disparity. I try to convince myself that reason should govern; look for motives to justify Henry's irrational actions. Then I realize I have no idea what drives me or anyone else to do the things we do, other than complex emotions which cannot be explained.

Henry

Henry doesn't leave Barkerville. He has nowhere else to go. He works odd jobs in the daytime. That is, when he can get out of bed. He spends his nights drinking heavily and steadily, often in one of the two Sporting Houses at the edge of the Chinese section of town.

He realizes now it was a mistake to approach Laura. He returned only because he was goaded by a group of miners he met at Antler. They told him she was doing very well on her own; they made fun of his failure. He came back to claim what is legally his.

He now receives news of Laura from one of the Hurdy Gurdy girls. Laura has bought a new house. He knows why she moved. While she was at the hotel one night, he broke into her house and tore her place apart. She is scared. He has made her scared. He's pleased that he still has some power over her.

He's been living in a small cabin with Wei Ming, a miner he met on the road. He wonders if Laura knows that he's still in Barkerville. He watches her secretly. He has not been able to go and see Jake, afraid he might say something about — he doesn't even want to think about it. Drinking is the only thing that helps.

Some of the miners continue to goad him. He shouldn't have told them about Laura. He thought she'd take him back. Instead, he is nearly starving, while she owns property. The men laugh, just like he does at other miners whose wives leave them the moment their money runs out. It's commonplace. Too many men, too much money, and too few women. Whores, he thinks, all of them. Can be bought so easily. These thoughts fuel his nighttime binges. Lately, he's been getting too rough with the prostitutes. One of them has threatened to report him. But he pays them well.

When he first hears about Laura's upcoming birthday party at the Caller Hotel, Henry swears he won't go. He has avoided the hotel since his arrival — he doesn't want to see Jake and Laura together; to be made an even bigger fool in front of everyone.

The day of the party, Henry gets up at noon, opens a fresh bottle of whiskey and starts to celebrate early. In late afternoon, he falls asleep and re-awakens just past nine o'clock. He washes, puts on clean clothes, then goes to the Caller Hotel.

It's the first time he's seen Laura face-to-face since the night he left her old house. At first, he is content to watch her while sitting at a table in the saloon. She glances at him now and then, but keeps to the other side of the room. Henry drinks quickly and, the more he stares at her, the angrier he becomes.

When he finally gets up and begins walking towards her, she quickly turns and leaves the saloon. He feels dizzy and sits back down for a moment, to get his balance. To hell with her, he thinks. He wipes his arm across the table, pushing a full glass of whiskey onto the floor.

"Settle down, Henry," someone says. He lifts his head. He's been staring at the wooden floor, at the unbroken glass rolling back and forth in a small semi-circle. Empty and going nowhere.

He gets up slowly and leans into the next table. There are two pretty young women there and he grabs the elbow of one, trying to force her onto the dance floor.

"Let go of her," her partner shouts.

"Just a little dance. No harm." Henry continues to tug at the girl's arm. He focuses on the white skin under his fingers. Freckled and soft. His fingernails are black. He thinks he can smell her perfume. He watches a hand pry his from the girl's arm, then looks up. He hasn't noticed the two miners who now stand at either side of him. Menacing. He pushes one roughly aside and goes back to his table, shouting for another drink.

A man's voice close to his ear. "Come on, Henry. You've had enough. Time to sleep it off."

Laura and Jake stand by the doorway. Someone pulls Henry out of his chair and he doesn't resist, but walks meekly until he reaches Laura.

"Well, well, well." Henry stops. "Look at who's here." He speaks loudly; people are staring at him.

"Get out of here," Jake says quietly.

"Just as soon as I've had a word with my wife." He shouts the words so loud that everyone stops talking. They are all watching him, he thinks, waiting for him to do something. He frowns at their faces.

"Well, well, well," Henry says again with an ugly forced laugh. He leans close to Laura and peers into her eyes, then straightens. "Sorry folks. There's been some mistake." He waves his arms as if he were giving a speech. "I'm afraid this is not my wife. This," he says, pointing to her, "is a whore and that is her . . ."

Jake's fist hits his nose before he can complete the sentence. Laura screams and Henry laughs, falling backwards against her. He tastes blood and wipes his nose on his arm. Then he lunges at Jake, fists pounding. A small circle of men close in around them, excited, urging Jake on. Then Laura presses herself between them, shouting, "Stop," and Henry's fist hits the left side of her face by accident. She reels backwards and Jake catches her as she drops to the ground, his hand cradling her head. "Get some water, quick," he calls.

Henry wavers, uncertain, watching them both. Then he shrugs. "It's what she deserves anyway." He turns and walks out of the saloon.

Even after this incident, Henry refuses to leave Barkerville. He stays another month, sleeps during the day and skulks the saloons at night, begging old miners to buy him drinks. He eats Wei Ming's food and gulps his whiskey until Wei Ming tells him he'll have to find work or leave. He can sense hostility towards him wherever he goes. Sometimes, he tells himself he's imagining it, but there is no mistaking the fact that people no longer talk to him when he meets them on the street. And soon after, he begins to despair as one by one the saloon keepers bar him from their establishments.

He leaves Barkerville. With no destination, he simply keeps moving along the road until he finds miners working on a claim. He always gets work, as long as it's just for food and drink. He doesn't need any more than that.

He continues this vagabond existence for the next year and twice returns to Barkerville briefly to spy on Laura. He watches her from the clearing. Once or twice, he almost surprises her there.

It is from this spot that one day in September Henry watches Laura and Jake walk arm-in-arm to the stagecoach departing for Victoria. Jake bends and kisses Laura on the cheek, then he boards and waves to her. Laura pauses until the coach rounds a bend, then slowly walks back home.

Henry climbs down the hill and goes to buy some food and two bottles of whiskey. He chooses a Chinese shop where he isn't likely to be recognized, or at any rate, spoken about. Then he returns to his oasis on the hillside.

It has been a dry, hot summer. Dusty. Below him, the townspeople move quickly, and raise small puffs or long trails of dust with their bare feet, heeled shoes, or workmen's boots. Henry watches the swirling activity below; each rising and settling of dust so unique, yet unified. He longs to be a part of something. As mid-day approaches, more people come out onto the streets. Women march arm-in-arm along the boardwalks, parasols leaned against their shoulders as stiffly, Henry thinks, as rifles. In the doorway of Moses' barbershop are men who Henry knows are waiting as much for news as for haircuts. Moses keeps a diary in which he documents all the events of the town. Henry wonders if there is any mention of him in that diary. To one side of the barbershop, several small boys are kicking stones against the back wall of a house. He starts to watch the stones, imagining the thud against wood, and sometimes thinks he sees marbled fool's gold glinting in the arch of dusty clouds made by the boys' kicks. Circles and cycles. Footsteps; prints. Even the horses leave their traces. More than anything, Henry wants to belong, to leave a part of himself in that dust below. It seems he is always on the perimeter of things, always watching and never participating.

At mid-afternoon, he eats the food, then opens the first bottle. Laura has not come out of her house all day. He plays a game, imagining what she is doing. Sewing, perhaps. Then building a cooking fire. Scrubbing potatoes and carrots. He sees her face at the window for a moment, just after she lights the lamps at dusk. Now she is eating dinner. And later, she'll settle by the fire with a book. He takes a swig from the whiskey bottle. Memories come and go. He knows her so well, he thinks, that he can see her behind closed curtains.

He drinks a quarter of the whiskey and falls asleep. When he awakens, the night is cold and frosty. He checks his pocket watch. Four-twenty. Below him the town sleeps. In the darkness Henry can see a twinkle of sparks rising from every chimney. Some alight on roofs and linger for a moment before going out. Soon the snow will form a soft carpet for those sparks. Henry shivers and wraps his blankets closer. He should build a fire. He pulls out his tobacco pouch and papers, and deftly rolls a cigarette. He lightly taps the end against his hand, lights it, inhales deeply, and lies back on the ground, eyes closed. He should have gathered more firewood, he thinks, remembering the three or four small pieces beside him — pieces left over from a previous fire. The last time he came back, it was too dry for him to risk building an open fire. He shivers again. His mouth is parched and dusty. He sits up and reaches for the whiskey bottle.

All around him, the sky shines with Northern Lights. Parallel rays shoot upright in the west, east, and north, making the frosty branches around him sparkle like sugar clusters. Henry watches as he has on many other nights. The rays, buffeted by the cold south wind, waver and snake, then diffuse into a radiance of ever-changing shapes, growing so bright that Henry can clearly see Barkerville below him. At times, the rays dissolve into blackness only to reappear as bright, brighter than before, phosphorous colors all pointing, Henry imagines, to Laura's house. The rays are a sign, he tells himself, aiming, showing him the way. He drains the remainder of the first bottle. His limbs are stiff with cold, though he feels flushed and hot inside. He stands and stretches, shaking the dust from his clothes. If he is going, it'll have to be now, before dawn, while the town still sleeps. Inside his belly, a burning sensation begins. Maybe he should just stay here and watch the sun rise above the mountains. No. He has thought about it long enough. Later today, he'll leave the Cariboo and, with it, the memories and heartaches he has accumulated over the past few years. He uncaps the second bottle and drinks greedily, then leaves his pack on the hillside and takes only the bottle as he slowly descends into Barkerville.

He's surprised at how easily the door gives way and he feels a twinge of anger, irritation, that she has placed herself in such a vulnerable position. He's in her sitting-room. Accustomed to the darkness, he can see the black round shape of the stove huddling in the center of the room. He walks around it to its mouth, and stares at the glowing embers that cast warm reddish hues on his bare hands.

He's never seen the inside of her new house, although it is

much as he imagined it. He stands motionless, listening. The house is quiet except for the intermittent sound of sparks exploding up the chimney. He hears his own breathing and tries to control it by holding his breath. One, two, three, four, five. Releasing it. One, two, three, four, five. Filling his lungs. One, two, three, four, five. He sits down in a chair by the fire and warms himself while his breathing calms. He tilts his head back and lets whiskey roll down his throat. Warm and sticky. This is where he belongs. This should have been his house. Laura is sleeping in the next room. For a moment, he thinks he should leave now, but he makes himself remain, still and quiet. He waits too long. A calm settles in him and his head feels clear. He gets up slowly and tiptoes into her bedroom.

Laura lies on her back, breast rising and falling in small swells under her nightgown. Again, Henry feels the irritation. It is almost too easy.

He has his hand over her mouth and her arms pinned to her sides before she can utter a cry. Her eyes are wide and afraid; he is calm, in control. Excitement stirs him. He's never seen Laura as frightened and helpless as she is now. He lets out a soft laugh.

"So, who's calling the shots now?" he says.

She tries to bite into his hand, but he presses his wrist against her throat until she stops.

"No use struggling," he says. "It's been a long time coming. You're nothing but a little whore." He climbs over her on the bed and pins her elbows under his knees. With his free hand, he rips the front of her nightgown, then leans back staring at her small white breasts. She tries to raise her head and shoulders, teeth again biting into his hand, while small sounds emit from the back of her throat. He laughs, loudly this time, and hits her hard in the face so she falls back, limp, onto the pillow. He rips off her clothing and claws at her, his nails digging into her flesh. He wants to savor her fear, but she lies limp, eyes shut.

His own voice sounds foreign to him. Savage rasps, "I hate you. I hate you," like a mantra. Then, he shudders against her and lies still. His breath comes in heavy bursts. It is done, he thinks. But there is no exhilaration. What did he expect? Pears of sweat roll down his temples; he thinks he'll suffocate. Then suddenly a cold sensation overcomes the heat in him. He shivers. His stomach begins to churn and he leans over the side of the bed and vomits. He rolls off Laura and clumsily tries to cover her with the blanket. Her eyes are open and dull.

He sits in front of the fire and throws in pieces of kindling, one after the other, until the room is ablaze with light and the sparks sound like gunshots in his ears. He waits, he doesn't know what for, piling more and more wood into the stove, as if he can burn away what he's done. He takes the bottle of whiskey from the floor where he left it, and hurls it into the fire. It explodes and small shards of glass spray the room, imbed themselves in his arms. The stings of pain propel him to the door, out and onto the hillside. He reaches his hideaway and lies face down in the dust. Within moments, shouts and cries reach him from the town below. He raises his head and looks.

A column of smoke is rising from the roof of Laura's house. Henry watches as flames flare onto the shingles and, in less than two minutes, ignite the saloon. The wind carries a shower of sparks across the street, to settle onto roofs there. Within minutes, both sides of Main Street are aflame, hissing and crackling. Men and women carry what possessions they can away from the roaring sheet of fire which travels from roof to roof, burning everything in its path.

Laura

Laura feels herself being lifted from the bed in someone's arms; carried out of the burning house in smoke thick and blue. She is strangely disassociated from the strong arms around her, from the cries of distress that reach her as though through glass. She feels no pain, as if her body were not her own. She is carried outside and set down a little way up the hillside. She remains sitting there and looks, bewildered, around her. Men and women run, arms filled with blankets, trinkets, clothing. Farther down the street, she can see a human chain — men passing kegs of blasting powder from hand to hand, from the storehouse to a safe place on the hill. Now and then, someone shouts at her to get up, to help, or to ask if she is all right. She sits and stares.

She remains there until an explosion of coal oil tins knocks her to the ground. She stands up slowly then, and begins to walk along the side of the hill. No one pays her much attention. She walks, looking at the bundled possessions, thinking of the absurdity of some of the items that have been taken out for safekeeping. At the side of one such pile, she sees a pistol. She stoops to pick it up, then walks among the debris with it in her right hand. She climbs the hill.

She sees Henry before he sees her, there, in her private space. She walks towards him slowly with the gun pointed at his head.

He stares back at her without defending himself. His eyes are rimmed in red and his cheeks wet. When she is six feet from him, she stops and cocks the pistol. He remains still and, in his eyes, she sees no fear. She advances until she is less than a foot from him. Her finger caresses the trigger. He waits, his eyes unwavering, and suddenly she sees how weak and demanding he is. Even this, he expects from her. She drops the pistol at his feet, turns and walks back down the hill. Moments later, she hears the shot, freezes for a moment in mid-stride. Then she continues down the hill towards the inferno below.

PREMISE:
The Discovery of the Diaries

Victoria, B.C.
May 26, 1987

Detective Paul Evans
RCMP Detachment
Prince Rupert, B.C.

Dear Detective Evans:

I have read the manuscript with interest. It appears to be researched and certainly follows the historical events of that area. It brought back a lot of memories — confused recollections of things my mother told me about Barkerville where she grew up. However, although the characters' names are those of my ancestors, I don't know if their stories unfolded in the way described here.

My mother, Catherine, was born in 1869 (the year following the fire) and her mother died shortly thereafter. She was cared for by Jake Calder. She rarely spoke to me about her mother, saying that she'd never known her and knew even less about her father who, she told me, had died before her birth. This manuscript interprets these occurrences but I can't testify to its accuracy. It is most curious that someone would take such an interest in my family.

Please keep me informed on any developments. I will look through my mother's papers in the hope of discovering something.

Sincerely yours,

Timothy Andrews

Paul frowns. He and Annie are sitting in the Quesnel airport — a small square room — waiting for the Rent-a-Car which was supposed to be here on their arrival.

"Are you sure we're not supposed to go and pick it up?" he asks her, irritated. He's been up since six this morning. They took the morning flight to Vancouver and had to wait until four forty-five for a connection. It's now past seven, they haven't had supper yet, and they still have a sixty-mile drive to Wells.

"I've got the telex right here," Annie answers, patting her briefcase but not opening it. "Relax. It'll be here. You know how small towns are."

She's reading a book called *Barkerville*, which she bought in the coffee shop. Stacks of them next to the till. Paul wonders how she manages to stay calm, patient. She looks fresh and unruffled. He feels grimy, tired.

The car finally arrives; a few apologies, then they're on their way. They buy two wrapped sandwiches in the coffee shop; will eat a real dinner when they get there.

Paul settles back into the passenger seat and lets Annie drive. He closes his eyes but doesn't sleep. He thinks instead about Timothy Andrews' letter. A real disappointment. He was hoping for some link. Then he wouldn't have had to make this trip.

He sighs.

"You asleep?" Annie asks.

"If I were, I'd be awake now."

"I heard you sigh."

"I was thinking it would soon be over. Someone's bound to remember who she was. Then I can take my holidays."

She laughs. "I don't know why you stay in Prince Rupert if you hate it so much."

"Why do you stay?"

"It's a place. I'm not constantly trying to get out of it."

"No." Paul watches her drive. "What made you go there?"

She shrugs. "Job. Why not? One place is the same as the other."

"I guess," he says, unconvinced.

They arrive in Wells a little past nine. Annie misses the turn-off up the hill and stays on the highway, past the motel, the restaurant, the police station. In less than a minute there are no more lights.

"You missed it," Paul says. "It was back there on the hill. Turn around."

Annie slows the car. "I've got to find a place. There's got to be a side road somewhere."

"Just make a U-turn. It's not exactly rush hour."

She stops on the shoulder and does as he asks. They drive back a quarter mile and this time she turns right at the hill. On the crest, they see the Jack of Clubs Hotel. She parks the car in front of it.

"I'm starving," Paul says. "Let's see if there's a dining room."

The lobby is deserted. Paul stands at the front desk, calling, "Hello? Anyone there?"

An old man limps out of a side door, after what seems like an hour. "You want rooms?" he asks.

"Two singles. You got a dining room here?"

The old man laughs. "Coffee shop. Not open past lunch though." He opens the register. "Names?" and writes slowly, in round large letters.

"Anywhere else we can get supper?" Paul asks.

"You'll pay in advance. Twenty-eight dollars each room. That's not counting the tax." The old man looks at his watch. "The Hideway stays open till ten unless it's real slow. Down on the highway. You can't miss it."

Paul drives this time, back down the hill to the restaurant. It's a log building, wooden tables and chairs. Cozy. They settle into a booth near the door.

"A lot of people come through here?" Paul asks the waiter, after they've ordered dinner.

"Depends the time of year. It's starting to pick up now."

"Been here a long time?"

"Five years. Helped build it." He points to an area beyond the main room. "Putting in an addition right now. You folks visiting someone?"

"Not really," Paul says. "We're trying to find someone."

"Well it shouldn't be too hard if it's a local you're looking for. What's the name?"

"Ah, if we had that, we wouldn't be here."

Annie frowns at Paul. "We're looking for a young woman who may have come here last December," she tells the waiter. "Perhaps you'd remember? She seems to have made some friends here."

"Too long ago. We live month-to-month, you know. I really don't remember anyone specific. December. A lot of people come up here then. Visiting for Christmas and all that. What does she look like?"

"We don't know exactly," Annie says, and bites her lip.

The young man watches them curiously. Paul wonders if he thinks them odd looking for someone whose name they don't know, whose appearance they don't know.

"She's a friend of a friend," he lies, then thinks this sounds even more implausible. "Do you know someone here called Gus?" he asks.

"Gus. Gus. I don't think so. But I don't know everybody. Most people though." He smiles.

"What about Bridgit or Nancy and Joseph or Steve? Any of those names ring a bell? Bridgit might have had a ski rental business."

The young man shrugs. "I don't remember any Bridgit. That's a name you'd remember. Nancy, I don't know. There's a Nan, it could be her. Steve and Joseph, well those are common names. Several around here."

"What about a couple? Nancy and Joseph."

He thinks for a moment. "I don't think so. Although it's hard to say. After spring break-up (and I don't just mean the weather), people split. It's a long winter up here, snowed in and little to do. They may have been here then but there's no couple with those names here now."

They eat their dinner in silence, Paul annoyed because Annie said he sounded like someone conducting an inquisition. When they're back in the car, she says, "We'll do some checking at the hotel tomorrow. Someone's bound to remember her."

Paul nods. As they walk up the wooden steps in front of the hotel, he can hear the jukebox in the pub. For a moment, he thinks that if he were to go in, he'd find her sitting at a table, laughing among friends. He wishes he knew what she looks like.

He gets up at seven-thirty the next day, knocks on Annie's door and waits for her downstairs in the coffee shop. After breakfast, Paul goes to the front desk of the hotel and asks to see the register for last December.

The young woman is indifferent to his prying. Once he shows her his credentials, she flips the book around for him to see, and leans over the counter. Paul runs his finger along the names. There are only four women's names there, all of which the young woman dismisses because she knows them.

"What's she done?" she asks, interested. "Is she a criminal or something?"

Paul shakes his head. "Missing person, that's all."

"Imagine, her being here and all. Nothing much happens in Wells."

Paul smiles and thanks her. She gives him the names of two motels and another hotel, converted from a hospital. "Mostly monthly tenants in winter, though," she says. "We don't get a lot of visitors till summer."

Back in the coffee shop Annie is still reading her Barkerville book. He gives her the name of the hotel and they split up, each to get what information they can.

Paul walks down to the motel in the cool May air. They told him it could still snow. Last year, they had a blizzard in June. He wonders what makes people live in such a small, isolated community, with little industry except tourism in the summer. Well, he thinks, he stays in Prince Rupert. He shouldn't be one to judge.

At the first motel, a man greets him warmly. He's chatty, happy to have someone new to talk to. He remembers a young couple staying at the other motel.

"They were here just before Christmas. I only remember them 'cause they stopped by the gas station where I work and asked about getting to Barkerville. I told them there was nothing there in the wintertime, but they were bent on going anyway. They only stayed a couple of days, if that. The second day, she came in asking if she could rent skis. But this is no city. And I told her so."

"What did she look like?" Paul asks.

"It's been a while. Average, you know. Wore a hat the whole time, so I can't even tell what color hair. But I remember she had real light skin, but maybe that was because the guy she was with was real dark, like maybe he could have had some Indian blood in him. You oughta check at the motel. Maybe they remember her better."

Paul thanks him and walks to the other motel, the one they passed on the highway. He wonders if it was her. But if it was, it certainly does not agree with the entry in the diary. At the other motel, the owner shows him the register. There are many entries in the month of December. Paul jots down all the names for future reference.

He meets Annie back at the coffee shop and they discuss their findings over lunch. She has nothing to report. The hotel's had only regular guests this winter.

After lunch, they drive back to Quesnel and take the evening flight to Vancouver.

Helen Andrews.
Deceased 1962.
Apparent suicide.

The file is open on the desk in front of Paul. He stares at the latest note he made after checking with Victoria. He frowns, flips through the Timothy Andrews letter and re-reads it. No mention of suicide. Natural, he thinks, for a father not to want to remember that detail.

"We were living together. Helen and me, in one of those rooming houses. Torn down now." Mrs. Chambers carefully pours tea into two cups, and hands one to Paul. "Nothing permanent any more. Nothing to show for where we've been. Do you know, my old elementary school burned down?" She settles back into the couch.

Paul nods, sympathetic. He watches her beside him, a large woman with plump arms and dimpled hands, holding what Paul sees as a ridiculously small tea cup by the handle.

"Helen's parents were very traditional. Father a lawyer; mother a housewife. She never fit in. But then, what kids do?"

Paul sips his tea slowly. He's been very lucky to locate Mrs. Chambers. He called all the girls in Helen's graduating class in the hope that someone had maintained contact with her. "What can you remember about her?" he prompts.

"She was an average girl. You know. We all were. I hadn't seen her for a few years after high school. We met up again about a year before she died. More tea?" She leans forward, puts her cup down, and takes the tea cozy off the pot. Paul lets her top up his cup. He's hardly had time to drink any.

"The suicide," he says. "Sleeping pills, wasn't it? Were you the one who found her?"

"Good gracious no. She'd moved out by then. Heard it happened in a hotel room. Downtown, I think. You know. One of those places where the winos live. Helen," she says, leaning confidentially towards Paul, "was not someone I'd have pegged to do something like that. She was very reasonable. Do you know, I never saw her cry, not even about the adoption."

"The adoption?"

"Well you know, she couldn't very well keep the baby. Nowadays, maybe it wouldn't matter any, but in those days, well, she just couldn't."

Paul remains silent, thinking about this new information. He doesn't want to appear too anxious. "Did you know the father?" he asks.

"No. That was before we met up again. And she didn't want to talk about it. Her parents didn't know."

And probably never did, Paul thinks. "She must have been a very troubled young woman."

"Afterwards, well, that's what I said to myself. Maybe I could have helped her, if I'd known. But like I told you, Helen always acted like she was in control of everything. Who knows what goes on inside people."

"You wouldn't remember about the baby, would you? Who adopted it?"

"It was a girl, that's all I know. I don't think even Helen knew who adopted her. I think she had to sign a paper saying she wouldn't try to find her."

"Thank you very much, Mrs. Chambers. You've been a great help." Paul stands up and takes his jacket from the back of a chair.

"There is just one thing," Mrs. Chambers says as she lumbers to her feet. "The only reason I remember it, is because it was the only sentimental thing I ever saw Helen do."

Paul stops. "Yes?"

"Well, she had a keepsake box. It was an Indian thing, you know, made out of one piece of wood all bent around corners. Had carvings all over it. I think she said it was her grandmother's. Well, she kept things in it and often sat and read through whatever was in there." Mrs. Chambers smiles apologetically. "Of course, I never knew what was in there. It was private, you know?"

Paul nods.

"Well, when she was leaving, after she'd had the baby, she says to me, could I take the box to the adoption agency and ask it be given to whoever adopted her daughter. Well, I said why didn't she go herself? And Helen said she couldn't but that the box was like an inheritance."

"And did you deliver the box?"

Mrs. Chambers nods. "I did. But I don't know if it was sent on to the baby or not. I like to think it was."

Paul presses her hand. "Thank you. And if you think of anything else, please call."

Victoria, B.C.
June 17, 1987

Detective Paul Evans
RCMP Detachment
Prince Rupert, B.C.

Dear Detective Evans:

I've spent a considerable amount of time digging through boxes of old papers which I kept after my mother passed away. I've found something which may be a link — a builder's receipt for work completed on a house on Porcher Island — and am enclosing a photocopy of same.

I've been thinking about this and seem to recollect my mother telling me about a servant she had, Liza, or some such name, for a time. I believe the house was given to her for her services.

I'm sorry I can't be more specific about all this, but these things happened so long ago and my memory is not what it used to be.

I'll look forward to any further developments at your end.

Sincerely yours,

Timothy Andrews

Paul steers the rented power boat across the harbor. He's going to Porcher Island alone, on his weekend off. He doesn't want to scare her with uniformed policemen and confusion.

"I'm going fishing for the weekend," he told Annie yesterday. "Got to get away. Clear my head."

Of course Annie knows about the letter and the building receipt. Annie knows as much as he does because she was the one who made all the inquiries and tracked down the Porcher Island house which had once belonged to Philip and Catherine Andrews.

"An Indian family's been living in it since 1910. Names of Ward and Williams," Annie said. "They say it's been deserted since last November when the grandmother died. She was a kind of matriach, I gather. Was born in the house and never left. Her daughter looked after her in her later years. There are grandchildren spread out — have their own families — one in Terrace, one in Williams Lake, and one grandson in Winnipeg. Now what do you suppose all this has to do with Philip Andrews?"

Paul could only shrug when she told him this. But now, he's trying to piece things together. He thinks about the legend — the abandoned baby girl in the canoe who was washed up on the shores of an island. It's beginning to sound familiar. Whoever she is, Paul thinks, she is recreating the legend; following a predestined path. Or perhaps she has created the legend to coincide with the events in her life. He is beginning to think that she has devised a puzzle for him to solve; it is as if she were luring him, but to where he's not sure.

It takes him a little over two hours to reach Porcher Island. Ten forty-five. The tide is in (he checked the tables yesterday) and he is able to go up Humpback Creek and tie up to the dock in front of the house.

There is no reply to his knock and he waits only a moment before turning the doorknob.

Inside, he tiptoes among furniture, feeling like a voyeur. The grandmother died last November, but although the dust and the musty smell tell him that no one lives here now, he sees evidence that someone has been here, certainly within the past six months. There is fresh wood stacked neatly by the fireplace. In front of the window facing the dock is a large armchair and on its seat cushion lies a half-finished baby's sweater — one knitting needle still threaded, the other hooked through a ball of yellow wool. Paul touches it, then pulls back his hand, as if he is suddenly aware that he is intruding; that these are the intimate webs of someone's life.

The silence is unsettling. He walks throughout the main floor of the house. In the kitchen, he finds cupboards full of dry goods; dishes, cups, all tidily put away; on the wood stove, a coffee percolator. It is as if someone were about to return.

Paul climbs the stairs to the attic. Two small bedrooms with slanted ceilings. The first one has a bed, dresser, and a small desk pushed against the window. He enters eagerly. On the desk, there is a bentwood box, about a foot square. He opens it slowly and sees a diary lying on top of a stack of looseleaf papers. There are several sheets of blue-lined paper inserted in the diary. He glances at the dates of these. February last. Recent entries. He takes the box with him downstairs into the kitchen and lays it gently on the table.

She has left him another clue. He takes a deep breath. "Don't be silly," he hears Annie saying in his head. "She doesn't know you. This has nothing to do with you."

Paul fills the stove with wood and starts a fire. In one of the cupboards he finds a tin of coffee and, after rinsing out the percolator, he puts some in along with water, and sets the pot on the stove. It is only then that he sits down in front of the box.

It is made, as Mrs. Chambers said, out of one piece of wood, nicked and coaxed by steam to form corners. All four sides are intricately carved with figures of men, animals, birds, and sea creatures. Paul turns the box around and studies each side — the head of an eagle in profile; a woman with a sea otter swimming in her belly; a half-grizzly bear, half-man with a dorsal fin on its back; and a blackfish on the water, carrying a woman whose arms are clasped around a loon's feet. Just as the legend described.

TEXT:
*The Diaries
of Elise*

Porcher Island, February 3, 1987.

The house is empty as I am. There are only echoes of the past and drops of rain drumming against the window. The diary is all that's left of last summer. I re-read it often, to remind myself it happened.

I've been thinking about my great-grandmother, Catherine. We are so alike. Did she sit here and wait in this same chair? There are too many questions, too many reflections. I think I will go mad with thoughts. Are these similarities to do with blood? Or is our strongest connection the fact that we're both women trying to deny our inner feelings. Have I ever been content? This paper is smooth and fragile between my fingers, as brittle as we are. Both unsure, no better, no different in our yearnings. Perhaps what we fear most is that we can take ridiculous chances with our emotions and still survive, scarred but intact. And later we'll recall only one or two vivid moments.

I remember the exact moment we met. Did it even happen? His eyes too familiar and strange. Perhaps I've imagined it all. Those days captured in a moment which lingers like the intoxicating scent of firewood on a mountain trail. I keep retracing my steps along that path where the flowers never wilt, never fade.

I still have David's letter. The one he wrote me when we were strangers.

> *"Mid-July would be best . . . they live on Porcher Island . . . Fly into Prince Rupert . . . Let me know the exact date so I can meet you and take you out. It's only accessible by boat . . . ."*

I've read it so often, I don't need to look at the paper any more. I hear his voice saying the words. My mind, his words. But I like to pull the letter out and look at it. It assures me that David is real; that I haven't made him up, too.

✧

Porcher Island, July 8.

I met him today. Turn back time. He is not Nathaniel; hardly has any Indian features. His eyes are two black holes which threaten to suck me inside.

We rode in a small boat, in air thick with moisture, under a canopy of clouds which blended into the shoreline. In the ashen landscape, only David and I were in color, vivid as the life-preservers that lay in the bottom of the boat.

He talked of Winnipeg, used the "we," although he never mentioned his wife by name. I also said "we" when speaking of Vancouver. A small word to create boundaries for comfort. I told him about Catherine; he told me about Sarah.

Just past three hours, the dark shape of land loomed like a giant sea-monster floating on its back. Up ahead, the fade-in of the house. I knew what to expect, had read about this house with its steep roof and large window facing the dock. About Catherine sitting in that window waiting for Nathaniel. She is our great-grandmother. A root connecting us.

Framed in the window of the dark, weathernworn wood, a woman.

"It's Sarah," David explained. "She always sits there."

"A beacon," I said, thinking of Catherine. "To guide the loved ones home."

"What a romantic." David smiled. "She sits there so she can see everything and everyone."

"And be seen," I insisted.

"And be seen."

He stepped onto the dock and moored the boat. Then he held out his hand to help me out. His skin was smooth and warm and I left my hand in his long after I had both feet on the dock. He let go, picked up my suitcase, then led the way.

I watched him from behind: tall and slender. Imagined

workouts at a gym back in Winnipeg; wondered what his wife looks like.

When he turned to me as we stepped off the dock, I felt exposed, and hurried past him a few steps up the wooden boardwalk to the house, then stopped to wait.

"I won't bite you," he said. "Come on and meet Sarah and my mother, Pearl."

Sarah is seventy-seven, wrinkled and ruddy like a tomato picked green and left to ripen on a window sill. Most startling are her blue eyes, Catherine's eyes, my eyes. Sarah's are wider set — the only difference.

Sarah is a dock watcher. She knits constantly there, the needles like extensions of her hands. "They all gotta go past here, you know. I see it all. That dock's a great big fishin' rod — reels 'em in, throws 'em back out. I see it all. Ain't nothin' happens here I don't know about."

I wonder if I, too, will be thrown back out when my time ends.

After supper, David and I sat outside on the porch. The fog had vanished; the sky was bright with stars. It's been hot and dry the last two months, David told me. Fires rage all around.

After discussing the weather, we became silent. Perhaps he felt uncomfortable as I did; two strangers forced into intimacy. I made a joke of it and said, "Well, here we are on that desert island. Now what?"

"Tell me about yourself."

"There's not too much to tell."

After all the search through Laura's and Catherine's lives, my own story appears insignificant. I told him so. But he insisted. "We've got almost two weeks," he said. "Time enough for the other stories."

"Twelve days," I corrected.

I told him only my age, twenty-six, and said, "I'm a student of sorts. To support myself I do whatever's necessary." I purposely left out anything and everything about my personal life. I didn't tell him that I've never been married nor even thought about it; didn't mention Marc, my lover who moved in four months ago; didn't voice the regrets, the doubts; didn't give him any glimpses into my present. We are here, after all, to discuss the past. I have no place in it, not yet.

He laughed. "Brief and secretive."

"Your turn," I said.

"David Williams. Thirty-four. I teach Grade Twelve Social Studies in Winnipeg."

No details. I smiled though he couldn't see my face. Nearby, the hypnotic sound of frogs. Mosquitos. Black flies. David went inside to get a bottle of insect repellant. The air warm, humid. Moths fluttered in the shaft of light made by the open door.

When he returned, I recounted a brief version of Laura and Henry's story.

"How much of it is true?" David asked when I'd finished.

"What kind of question is that?"

"I just mean how can you be so sure of events that took place so long ago?"

"Oh, I'm sure, that's all." I stretched, yawned. Sitting there with him, I forgot who I was and imagined myself in that other time.

"But how did you piece it together, then?" he persisted.

I explained about the research, the notes in the bentwood box — all now a part of me. "And you will fill in the missing bits," I told him. "You and Sarah and Pearl."

We said goodnight on the porch. I went to my room and fell asleep trying to remember his face.

Porcher Island, July 9.

This morning, I awakened, disoriented, then suddenly remembered and a queasy feeling began inside me. My room is upstairs, next to David's. I breathed deeply, and made myself think of Marc.

Downstairs, there was coffee on the large wood stove. Pearl sat at the table, darning a shawl. I glanced around the room.

"He's out back, chopping wood," Pearl said, as if she'd read my thoughts.

I asked her about her family.

"Just Ma and me living here now," Pearl said. "And I wouldn't stay on if it wasn't for her. She's too set in her ways. Wouldn't hear of leavin'. Someone's gotta look after her." She finished darning a hole in the shawl and held it up. "Damn moths," she said. "Every winter they get worse." She nodded towards the living room. "She don't like the smell of moth balls. Says they stink like death."

David came in soon after and we sat with Sarah for a while, watching the dock. Against one of the walls in the living room is an old piano. Sarah noticed me staring at it and said, "One of 'em fancy women left that here. Old Lila used to plunk a few notes now and again."

Catherine, waiting for Nathaniel. Watching the dock, playing melodies for him into the night. At times, she awakened in her bed upstairs, perhaps the very bed I sleep in, and thought she heard sounds in the woods. She ran out in her nightgown calling to him. But it was only wind and squirrels, and, when Lila led her back to the house, she could not be comforted. Nathaniel simply vanished from her life as if he'd never existed. Only Sarah remained as proof.

Pearl told me she remembered a box filled with sheet music.

"Maybe in the shed," David said. "We'll go out and look

after lunch. How about a walk? I could show you where the frogs live. It's much cooler in the woods."

I agreed, delighted he suggested it, and ran upstairs to change into shorts, as excited as if this were my first date. I sat on the bed, grinning, chiding myself for being so foolish. But it's been so long since I felt this way. I can't remember who or when. Marc. For a moment, a tinge of guilt. Quickly shrugged off. Why worry about things that might never happen?

Outside, I settled into David's step; into his easy intimate manner. I can't begin to explain even to myself this feeling of recognition. Strangers who've known each other forever. We laughed. He showed me where he played as a child. I ran ahead of him and hid, then scared him from behind.

When we reached the marshy area, there was no sound of frogs croaking. Only the buzzing of dragon flies with large blue wings and slender black bodies. David said frogs sleep in the day, and I insisted he show me one, but we found none.

At the creek, we waded ankle-deep. The water was icy; numbed my feet almost immediately. David found a smooth rock on which we sat, back-to-back, while I told him a little about Catherine, a headstrong woman whose many defiances intrigue me. I gave him examples: she didn't marry until she was thirty-five; above Jake's objections, she chose a Victoria man; she volunteered her time at the Indian Hospital in Victoria, although her husband, Philip, did not think it suitable work for a woman in her social position; she befriended a young Indian woman, Lila, who became her constant companion; and she took a lover, Nathaniel, and bore him a child. Although David didn't dispute the last two, he did ask how I knew about the rest. I'd found some letters, I explained, and pieced it together. I told him that I'd brought with me four letters to Catherine from Philip, written during their seventeen month separation — when he was in Prince Rupert, and she in Victoria. Why she kept these particular letters, I'm not certain. I can only surmise that the country he described was Nathaniel's home and she was trying to preserve anything to do with him.

Porcher Island, July 9, 11 p.m.

This afternoon, when David and I returned from Humpback Creek, we rummaged in the shed. There were boxes and old trunks which I could spend days looking at. We found sheets of music in a cardboard box. Some of their corners had been nibbled by mice, some had faded so as to be almost illegible; all of them were damp and discolored. I turned each page gingerly until I found what I was looking for: the familiar handwriting, the words *Catherine Andrews* scrawled neatly in black ink.

Porcher Island, February 4, 1987.

It rains and rains. Will it ever stop? I look at these entries. It's all so obvious to me now. Why couldn't I see what was happening then? And Marc, what was he thinking during those months after I returned?

I remember a night. November. It must have been raining then, too. Vancouver. I'd been exorcising David with my pen. Scratching him loose from tight fissures, nebulous corners. I'd fallen asleep at my desk.

"It's three o'clock, for God's sake. Come to bed."

I awoke abruptly and raised my head. My arms were crossed over

the typewriter keys, and when I tried to read the last line I'd typed, I saw a series of odd letters: &xts
!0)i?uy$#wv'*oab.

Is this how it happened? *I shook my head, as if to scramble thoughts into order. It was too difficult to reconstruct lives, people. I knew their names, their mistakes. Now, I was trying to pump my blood into those names neatly scrawled by quills on old parchments. Perhaps I was trying to pump their blood into mine. But what did I know of their feelings, of their fears and hopes? I had trouble discerning the feelings of the man who slept in my bed.*

"*Elise?*" *Marc stood in the doorway.*

I kept my arms crossed over the typewriter.

"*Give it up,*" *he said.* "*It's the middle of the night.*"

I stared at him. What did it matter what time it was? Day, night, in this room with the windows shuttered, the right time was when I could think freely; when the typewriter could beat out my thoughts. Clack-clack, clack-clack-clack, clack-clack. I didn't want to be enslaved by the rhythm of the earth's movements, of Marc's schedules.

I never should have allowed him to move in. *We were happier before. I stifled myself mid-sigh. Marc's eyes were half-closed and he ran one hand over tousled hair while the other held up the waistband of his brown and white striped pyjama bottoms.* He is vulnerable. *I hated to see this side of him because it made me feel guilty, as if I were a monster slowly destroying him without his knowledge.*

"*All right, I'm coming.*" *I curled the left half of my mouth upward, like a smile.*

Marc returned to the bedroom, apparently satisfied. I took extra time tidying the papers on my desk, even though I knew it was ridiculous to do this because we'd rented this two-bedroom apartment so that I could have a private study.

But what did Marc know about me after all the time we'd been together? And what did I know about him? Intimate partners. No, there is no such thing. There are only individuals projecting their needs one onto the other. I can't stop thinking about intimacy, or its non-existence.

Porcher Island, July 10.

Only three days. Feels like much longer. Today David put into words what I've been feeling. We were lying on a blanket on the dock between swims. He was teasing me about the notebook I carry with me always. I told him I didn't want to forget anything. I was on my stomach, staring out at the water, trying to find words to describe its color — blue, green, and black all at once, with lozenges of gold floating on the wave crests which nestled gulls.

"Will you forget me," he asked. "unless you write me down?"

"Probably," I answered, teasing.

"No you won't." He said it so seriously that I lay my head down on my arms and closed my eyes so that he couldn't read anything in them. Eyes are too honest. Even through my closed lids, I could feel him watching me.

"Look at me."

I opened my eyes and saw that he too had laid his head down and was facing me.

"We may as well talk about it," he said.

"About what?"

"About whatever this thing is between us."

"What thing between us?"

"There's nothing wrong in admitting that we're attracted to each other."

"Oh. That," I said in a silly, casual way, as if it were a natural thing.

"Yes. *That*." He laughed. "So, what are we going to do about it?"

I shut my eyes again and thought about my answer. I felt disarmed by his honesty. As if he were breaking the rules to a game I hadn't quite learned. Finally, I said, "If there's one thing

I've learned through the years, it's not to give in to impulses."

He laughed and I opened my eyes. His were twinkling, triumphant.

"I'm serious," I insisted, annoyed.

His chest and arms were gold, like caramel. In the past three days, I have watched him turn darker every hour in the sun. More and more like Nathaniel. And I, white and burning, with Catherine's eyes, filled with her desires. I shook these thoughts out of my head, and turned to face the house. Sarah was plainly visible in the window, head bowed over the wool, asleep. When I turned back to him, David was staring intently at me, his face so close to mine I could smell the salty sea-water in his hair. "Do you have any idea," he said softly, "how much I want you?"

For a moment, I felt myself being pulled towards him, then I turned away.

He laughed and rolled onto his back. I stood up and dove into the cold water, annoyed with myself for having these feelings.

When I had dried off, I went inside to get Philip's letters to read to David.

June 1906

Dear Catherine,

We made it up here safe and sound although some of the men have colds as it hasn't stopped raining for weeks.

We arrived at the village of Metlakatla on May 7th and were fortunate to find a steam launch, the Constance, available. We hired a Captain Robinson who took us across to the proposed site.

The harbour is completely land-locked and appears to be of uniform depth. Toward the harbour mouth, the western shore is made up of a number of islands through which is Venn Passage. The islands all have rocky cliffs extending a few feet under the water, turning it the colour of green ivy. Then there is a sheer drop-off, at which point the sea turns black, so deep it must be.

The point we've chosen for the terminus is along the eastern shore of the harbour and is backed by two low mountains (Mount Olfield being one) which appear to descend straight into the sea. There is no level land.

We began construction on the 17th of May, with a tool shed (for we feared everything would turn to rust) and the erection of some tents for accommodation. We spent the next few days surveying for the dock and the Company houses. Since then, we've been clearing the foreshore and begun the building of the wharf.

The tents are cold and damp. A far cry from our home in Victoria. I do hope you're keeping well, Catherine, and have had no difficulties since my departure.

I fear I will be here a little longer than expected, but I'm sure you will understand. I will write again when the wharf is completed.

Philip

October 1906

Dear Catherine,

I apologize for not replying to your letters sooner, but I have been very occupied with the work here. I trust you received news of me via Mr. Cabot back in July.

I'll catch you up on our progress since my last letter. We completed the wharf as planned by July 1st. Much celebration followed this accomplishment. Next came the sleeping quarters (you'll be glad to know I'm no longer in a tent) and then the business of cutting a road through the wilderness from the wharf.

This road has been named Centre Street and is really just a narrow wooden boardwalk with hand railings. From it, branch out small walks which lead to temporary buildings on either side. The grade is so steep that we've had to install a narrow gauge railroad, up which a car can travel, to move heavy equipment and supplies. The buildings connected to the road are also on this irregular terrain. Adjacent structures have individual grades. Most are built on pylons, partly to even them out and partly to ward off the wet and damp. It is humorous to see the first floor of one building even with the roof of the next.

I've made quite a few friends. Most of the people here work for the Company, although there are a few independents who supply essential services, as well as a sawmill on the NE corner of the island at Seal Cove.

All the land here is owned by G.T.R., with the exception of an Indian Resevation south of Centre Street, which the Company is trying to buy.

G.T.R. has been trying to discourage settlers thus far. But a particularly resourceful man, John Knox, filed a mining claim and he and his friends have put up a number of temporary buildings on his claim — a squatter's community known as Knoxville.

Not much more to say, Catherine, except to hope that you will keep well until I next see you.

                              Philip

                            June 1907

Dear Catherine,

I was very glad to receive your last letter with news of Jake and all the people of Barkerville. Since coming here, I've begun to understand better the people of Barkerville. This place is similar, in that here too we are struggling to accomplish and build a dream. I've almost forgotten life in the city. Here each does his share, and we work side by side, regardless of status. I'm sure you would approve of my new friends. At night, I can look out westward from here and see the lights of the village of Metlakatla twinkling between islands. You've never thought me a sentimental man, I'm sure.
You'll be interested to hear that we're rather civilized by now. We have a bank — The Canadian Bank of Commerce — a drug store operated by a Mr. Reddie, the United Supply & Contracting Co. dealing in hardware and lumber, the Kelly-Carruthers Supply Co. dealing in general merchandise, L. Morrow & Co., a meat market, a barber shop run by Harvey Creech, two phsyicians — Dr. J.G. McKay and Dr. E. Tremayne (who is our company

doctor) and an Anglican Church. So you see, what started out as an idea has blossomed into quite a bustling community.

And now, dear Catherine, some happy news. I will be returning home in mid-September. However, I must add that I will have to return here by November as there is work which I've not yet completed. You have been so patient thus far, please bear with me a little longer. Soon, we shall have some happy weeks together and discuss future plans.

Philip

November 1907

My Dear Catherine,

It was wonderful to be home with you again, even if it was only for such a short duration. I'm very much looking forward to your arrival here. It's no easy task, this building of a city.

It seems since my departure, there has been some excitement in our small community. I think you will get enjoyment from this story.

I don't believe I've mentioned a Mr. John Houston before. He is a newspaper man whom you would get on quite well with, Catherine. He abhors the Federal Government and the policy of Grand Trunk with regards to Oriental labour. I can see if you were here, you two would become fast friends. He caused quite a stir when he arrived and took refuge in Knoxville. G.T.R., trying to keep him silent, refused to allow him to ship in a press. But Houston had one sent up anyway and, when it landed at the docks, G.T.R. seized it and locked it in a warehouse. Well, you can imagine how this was the worst thing they could have done. Houston marched up to the local constable and lodged his complaint and, before no time was up, the two of them were at the warehouse and had broken the lock on the door. With the aid of a few volunteers, they carried the press up Centre Street and positioned it in front of the Provincial Police Office, with a tent over it. And there, without further incident, the first issue of ''The Empire'' (as he named it) came to be published on September 21st. And, if this issue is any example, I can well see why G.T.R. tried their best to silence him.

I can almost see you smiling, Catherine, at the outcome of this story. There is freedom of the press even in such a remote place as this. I have grown very fond of it and of its people, many of whom have become my close friends.

I look forward to your letter. I trust Lila is well and has gotten over her flu.

Philip

Porcher Island, February 5, 1987.

I sit in Sarah's chair, Catherine's chair and stare at the dock. Waiting. Always waiting.

Son, Woman-of-the-Sea will return my bracelets. The child stirs in me, but she will be claimed. I cannot change the legend.

Two entries of the diary are missing. July 11 and 12. Did I even write them? Perhaps I tore them one night, while sitting at that desk in Vancouver, while Marc paced the floor around me, asking, "What's wrong? What have I done?" Or perhaps it was later, after Christmas, after I left David forever. What does it matter now? I know what happened. I made it happen. I'll make it happen again:

✧

Porcher Island, July 11 and 12.

A desperate longing, an inability to do much other than to be near David. I must have woven tales to keep him near me. I wanted so much to be accurate, to be sure not to misplace anything, not to forget. It doesn't matter. It's all so vivid. In my brain, a montage.

I keep pushing David out of my thoughts.

"I have a short memory. Rarely goes past three weeks."

Did he say that or did I?

"When I get home, I'll file you under Things That Never Happened."

I just can't remember. Did we both say it? Did either of us mean it? Were we being honest or dishonest? So many games, so many words are looped inside my head, I can't distinguish the tones. Have I made everything up? No, not everything.

Where is Marc? I need him here now. We've been together too long to risk parting. David weaves in and out of my dreams, creates unresolvable conflicts. It's better not to remember.

Marc and I sitting in the car while I watched landscape run past me. Trying to decide what to do about David, between fir trees. We were driving in the country. Marc made faces at me from his corner. He was being playful, growling, stroking my arm. I ignored him and continued to stare out of my half-open window at the trees which moved quickly beside me. We were each strapped to his place.

Marc pointed to the empty space between us. "Sit here," he said.

I shook my head. "I want to be by the window." I needed this distance.

The road was gravel; stones slapped against the bottom of the car. Another road. David was sitting beside me, in the passenger seat. The air was hot and dry. We trailed a cloud of dust thick enough to erase our tracks. He said, "Things will never be the same." I laughed and pretended not to understand the words he wrapped in humor.

"It's so beautiful," I said to Marc, clasping and unclasping the seat-belt. I imagined the trees running past me outside the car. But I couldn't stop the moment. I imagined Marc and me living here. A house in the forest, walks to the lake. There was a dam and signs: CAUTION. WARNING.

At the end of that other gravel road, we scaled the bank, reached the lake at the bottom of the trail. I wore sandals and he took my hand to steady me.

"We could buy a place," Marc said, taking my hand. "Could you stand being this far out in the wilderness?"

With *David*. On the lake, there were two canoes, a red and a yellow one. The beach was pebbled: flat, smooth stones. I scooped up ones that he could skip. Pants rolled to mid-calf, he waded in the black, icy water, calling me to join him. I laughed, avoided splashes, pulled the green sweater around my shoulders, sleeves knotted in front.

Later, during dinner, the red canoe moored across the lake. A plane trailed water, orange wings glistening in the heat. There were cigarettes and the chain of lakes. The air hazed blue, closing in.

After dinner, we drove the same dusty road, erased our steps.

I squeezed Marc's hand. He was real and solid beside me and when I looked through the rear window, I saw tire marks on gravel.

We must have spoken. David and I. All I remember are looks and laughter, Sarah, the dock. A haze of faces, meanings, music, and imagined frogs dancing on lily pads. We must have spoken things on these days I couldn't bear to record.

Porcher Island, July 13.

David and I walked up to Baker's place in early afternoon. Sun overhead; shadows puddled around our feet. Heat mirrored in an albescent sky. Twigs bleached grey. Even the swamp crackled, whined under our weight. Rusty veins cracked dry in earth. And dust. A fine layer that settled in our clothes, hair, nostrils, turning even beads of sweat into black drops trailing from our temples.

Baker's place was set a couple of miles inland. David said the creek dissected their land further up. "We can wash there," he said.

We stood in the water and washed our legs, arms, faces, necks, anything that was exposed. Then we stood and let the sun tingle us dry. From there, we could see the large farmhouse and, adjacent to it, the barn's A-frame. The roof was made of wooden shingles, sharp and fraying at the edges. Above the doorframe, the shingled teeth uneven, some missing — the mouth of an old woman.

David told me this barn was used for every social occasion in the area and on Sundays for religious services.

"Do you know everyone around here?" I asked.

"Just about. There may be a couple of new families, if they came after I left last fall. Most people, though, once they come here, tend to stay."

"You left," I said.

He began to walk without answering and I followed. We'd been invited to an afternoon salmon barbeque. Through the trees, I could see people carrying things to the barn. Women in long colorful skirts and men in checked shirts and jeans. Naked children with long hair pasted to their shoulders, along the length of their backs.

"A time warp," I said, more to myself than to David.

He turned and smiled. "Maybe we've just rushed ahead to other things too quickly."

I caught up to him and we stood together watching the scene. After a moment, David asked, "What's he like?"

"Who?"

"The other half of your 'we'."

"Oh . . . he's . . . nice," I concluded lamely. Then, "A great person." Guilty. "We get along very well." The solace of clichés. Difficult things made safe and familiar.

He didn't press me for details. Perhaps he understood I didn't want to talk about Marc, about anything in my other life. We knew nothing about each other.

"And what about her?" I asked. "What's she like?"

"Same." He touched my elbow. "Come."

And now I wonder if this absence of our recent pasts made us more similar. Edges glassed smooth so we could mirror each other. Should I have told him about Marc? About my fears, my feelings, myself?

He introduced me to people as we came upon them. Scrubbed faces, without makeup, long hair tied at the neck or cascading down a back — all similar and somehow familiar.

A beautiful young woman came running, threw her arms around David's neck. He held her while I busied myself staring at a handmade basket — staring through the lattices at the dry ground below. I listened to a detailed account of how it was made, listened without hearing the words. I was trying to read messages in their delighted looks, trying to decipher their moving lips.

Finally, he released her. Still holding her hand, he motioned to me, introduced us.

She smiled. "A cousin, I understand."

"Of sorts," I said.

"Isn't he a mysterious one? He never told me before."

Her voice scraped at something inside me. The smooth confidential tone. Intimate. It reminded me once more that I know nothing about him.

"Old lover?" I asked David when she'd moved away from us. I couldn't help myself.

"Not so old," he replied, laughing, avoiding my question.

The rest of the afternoon, a blur of smiling faces, soft voices, children's laughter. I distanced myself from David, all the while searching for him, trying to piece him together. Several times I saw their faces close, sharing things I could no longer even guess at. The scraping continued inside me, making thin paper cuts on feelings I was trying to disregard.

Then finally, the walk home. Just the two of us, alone. My head filled with questions I'd never ask. And if I did, he'd never answer.

✧

Porcher Island, February 6, 1987.

I've been falling asleep at odd times in the day, still sitting in front of the window. It rains. There is light. Darkness. Rain. Clouds. Moon. I've not been upstairs for a few days.

I am still thinking about intimacy. I have begun tearing apart the word, searching for meanings:

intimacy: in-team-a-sea
intimacy: I-untie-my-sea
intimacy: in-team-ace-I
intimacy: in-time-I-sigh
intimacy: in-time-icy
intimacy: in-time-I-see

Nonsense. The word and its meanings. Intimate. Add an "i" and a "d" and it becomes intim(id)ate. Similar words. The id. I and David added in between. I will go mad if I don't stop thinking.

Memories. Those twelve days split into separate eternities. Does he remember each one, I wonder? Or does one stagger into the other, like flowers planted at intervals through a season, some budding, some wilting, but some always in bloom?

It would be much easier to simply accept the changes — to let the pink moist petals lose their scent with the cooling of days, weeks, months; to enjoy their velvet textures, the pollen that clings sticky to fingers, then let them disintegrate without trying to press them raw between pages. It would be so much easier.

Instead, I prod my memories, find flat dried imprints and nurture them to blooms once more. I listen to every word, every phrase, the inflection and timbre of voices. It is all unchanged and it is still July in Porcher Island.

✧

Porcher Island, July 14.

I was sitting beside Sarah, doodling in my notebook, when suddenly she said, "You's always writing. I got to thinking 'bout Old Lila."

"What about her?" I asked.

"When I was a young'un, she used to write things down too."

"What kind of things?"

"I don't rightly know. I never learned to read or write proper. Though Lila, she tried to teach me times. I never had no head for writing." Sarah stopped clicking her needles and stared out at the dock. "You know something?" she said, patting my arm. "I nearly forgotten all them writings till now."

"What's happened to them?" I asked.

"They still 'round here someplace. If'n Pearl didn't throw 'em out or use 'em for kindling."

"What did they say?"

"What did what say?" She looked puzzled.

"The writings. Did Lila read them to you?"

"Na. They was private writings. Some folk, they can't talk themselves out so they get to praying and tellin' it to God. Other folk, they just keep birthin' so those hungry mouths suck the feelings out of 'em. Old Lila, she write it all down. She don't got no God and no young'uns."

I asked her to tell me a little about Lila. I know only what Catherine wrote about her. Sarah started knitting again, didn't answer immediately. I waited until she'd finished two rows before she spoke.

"She was like my mama to me, Old Lila. Always teachin' me something. She used to say, 'Sarah, you're different. You gotta learn proper ways.' Always talkin' about proper ways. She'd learned it from a white lady she tended across the water, before we come out here." She paused a moment. "That lady, she learned her a lot of stuff Old Lila never had no use for out here."

"Did you ever meet the lady?" I asked her, thinking of Catherine's teachings crossing the water through someone else.

"I never bin across the water," Sarah said simply. "Old Lila, she went across three, four times a year. Always come back with dresses and fruit." She stopped knitting a moment. "One time though," she said, "I was just a young'un then, but I remember a boat come up to the dock. Lady sitting in the boat, talking to Old Lila. Wearing a dress so green and shiny, you swore it was made of moss.

"Old Lila, she calls out to me to go see, but I went and hid outback till the tide come in and set that boat abouncing across the water again. Old Lila, later, she ask me, 'Why didn't you come?' I told her I was scared 'cause it looked like that lady's hair was on fire, it was so red and I didn't want it burning me too." Sarah chuckled. "After that, next time Old Lila went across, she come back with a picture book full of ladies with red and yellow hair. She says, 'Look, it's not burning, it's just different from yours and mine. Lots of people got different colors coming out of their heads.'" Sarah laughed, and I smiled to see her so happy. "Poor Old Lila. She never was good with learnin' me things. For a long time, I used to wake up in the morning and look to see if there was any colors comin' out of my head. It weren't till I was older that I knew what she meant."

I took her hand and we laughed together. Pearl came in and we stifled our giggles, as if we were guilty children. She said, "We already had breakfast. Coffee's on but I can cook you something if you like."

"No, just coffee's fine."

When I came back from the kitchen, Sarah was knitting again, and all the laughter had gone from her eyes. When she remembers things, it's as if she relives them, becomes whatever she was in the re-telling. I took my place next to her. I'm becoming attuned to the dock; to the sound of waves thrashing the pylons; to the constant click of knitting needles; to David.

Porcher Island, July 15.

Today, David took me out in the row boat. Sarah watched us from the window and, as we pulled away from the dock, I saw her dab her eyes with her fingers.

"She thinks you're leaving," David said.

The eighth day. I don't want to think about leaving. There are no loons in these waters.

When I told him the legend, David said I made it all up, but I could tell he wasn't certain. He tried to find examples to prove his theory. He said I'd modified real things and turned them into inventions. Like the two gold bracelets around my wrist; and my passion for skipping flat stones on the surface of the water; and the fact that I've planned to be on this island exactly twelve days. But I insisted that these are mere coincidences. The legend came first; because of it, we're here. I have not invented us, I reminded him. We're part of our past.

I brought my notebook with me in the boat. It has become a part of me, and David teases me constantly about it. He says, can't I just forget all that and enjoy? But I want to record each moment, each detail. I don't trust my memory. From the boat, I scrutinized everything: the water, black except where the sun was trapped on the crests of waves; the shoreline, jagged and rocky; large rocks protruding from the water like green-brown furry creatures which rose or buried their heads according to the tides; the mountains in the background, dark forests engulfed in the bluish haze of smoke; a lone eagle overhead, practicing maneuvers — like a figure skater in the air, backwards and forwards, turning lazy inside the wind's pockets. I could not have remembered these things if I had not written them down.

When he'd rowed for a while, David pulled in the oars and threw out his fishing line.

"Tell me about your father," I said, settling into the bottom of the boat, back leaning against one of the seats.

"If you promise not to scribble while I talk. I feel like I'm giving an interview."

I smiled and closed my notebook. I remember almost everything he told me.

Ironically, Samuel Williams came to Porcher Island to work in a gold mine. Do cycles ever end? David thinks he arrived around 1935 and worked at Surf Point Mines. He was of Irish descent, but was a native of California. He married Pearl near the end of the war. "He was a wandering man," David said. "After I was born, he left for good."

"You've never seen him since?"

"Wouldn't even know where to look."

We paddled to a small secluded inlet, then David pulled the boat up on shore and helped me out. He'd caught a salmon while we talked. He cleaned it quickly, expertly, with his pocket knife, while I gathered kindling. The driftwood was bleached white from the sun and I amused myself by picking pieces shaped like birds and fish. I carried an armload back, a dry and weightless menagerie, which I made David identify piece by piece before I let him make a fire of it.

"We're not really supposed to do this," he said. "It's been a long dry summer." From the trees nearby he cut even sticks, then laid them across the stones that circled the fire, to form a grate. He put the cleaned fish on top.

We sat a little away from the fire, bathing in the warmth of the early afternoon sun. An orange water-bomber circled overhead, then released a waterfall from its gills, trying to quench the forest's thirst.

While we waited for the salmon to cook, David told me the legend of Gitrhawn (Salmon-Eater.)

"A real one," he said. "Not like the one you made up." And when I tried to object, he silenced me with a grin. "Imagine," he said, "an elderly Chief who had many wives, one of whom was a beautiful, clever young woman. Imagine a young handsome prince, the nephew and successor to the elderly Chief."

"I imagine there will be trouble," I said.

"Imagine," he continued, "an Eagle which the young woman trained as her pet and kept with her always. Imagine two copper bands around each foot of the bird. A little like these." David lightly fingered the gold bracelets around my wrists.

"You still think I made it up, don't you?" I said. "Well, I didn't. All the things you mentioned are quite commonplace in legends. And fairytales."

"Hush. How will I ever tell you the story if you keep interrupting?"

"O.K. I promise not to say another word."

"As you rightly guessed, the trouble began when the young woman and the young prince fell in love and started to meet secretly, whenever the elderly Chief was away.

"The Chief, who was a great hunter, noticed that suddenly many of his snares were empty and that he was not able to bring home as much game as he had formerly.

"The Chief suspected that all was not right at home. But when he returned, he found nothing out of the ordinary because, although the household knew of the young lovers' passion, they justified it by saying that when the Chief died, the nephew would inherit the young girl anyway. But the Chief was not so dense that he didn't suspect something. Therefore, he told his wife that he was going on a long hunting trip but in fact went only to the outskirts of the village, and there hid for part of the night. Then, just before daybreak, he sneaked back to his house and found the two lovers in his bed."

"Well, what did he expect anyway? You said yourself he was elderly and she was beautiful and young . . ."

"So he took out his knife, killed his nephew, then cut off his head and threw the rest of the body into the river. He hung the Prince's head over his doorway for all to see. The next day, he wrapped his wife in robes, put her in a box, laced the box up, and put it in a canoe. He then set the canoe adrift in the same waters as he had thrown the body of her lover."

"That's horrible! How could he do that if he really loved her?"

"He could have killed her, but he didn't."

"A high price to pay for passion," I said. "Dead or drifting until death on the sea. It doesn't seem fair, really."

"That's neither for you nor me to decide. This is the way the legend goes. I believe there was a box cast at sea in your legend too, wasn't there?" His eyes were mischievous, laughing at me.

"Completely different circumstances," I said. "In mine, there was a baby. An innocent baby."

"Aha! So you're judging the girl as guilty too."

"I didn't say that. I only meant they're two completely different legends, different characters and different names."

"Anyway, this young princess, much like your baby girl, traveled across the seas and also landed on an island. She was weak but alive. Flying overhead was her Eagle pet. And in this legend also, a Chief found the young princess. Although this Chief made her his bride."

"You know what I think?" I said suddenly. "I think *you're* the one making this up. Are you trying to tell me something?"

"What do you mean? I'm trying to tell you a real legend."

"I think not." I thought about what he'd said for a moment, then asked, "Do you know something about Nathaniel that you're not telling?"

"Now how did Nathaniel get into this legend? You're impossible. Always interrupting. How can I tell you anything?"

"The young prince had his head cut off." I thought of Catherine waiting for Nathaniel day after day, for months, but he never came to her, although she was having his child. "Who told you this legend?" I asked David.

"Lila. When I was just a boy. She knew all the old traditions."

"Maybe there was more truth to this legend than you think," I said. "Maybe she made it up to tell you something else."

"It's an old legend," he said stubbornly. "You'd find it written up if you looked. Besides, I think you're taking this too far. Everybody making up everything. Why can't you just accept information and leave it at that?" He stared at me. What really happened on that island? I can't even trust my memories.

"O.K.," I said, finally. "It's an old legend."

"Come on, Gitrhawn," David said smiling. "The salmon is ready to eat." He used two sticks as tongs and handed me some.

We ate with our fingers while sitting side by side on a fallen tree. David showed me how to pull the bones out all at once. The salmon was moist and tasted of fire. When we finished eating, we went to the water's edge and washed our hands and faces, the salt stinging our eyes.

"Let's go for a swim," he said. But I had no bathing suit and the water was cold. "You'll warm up in the sun. We'll skinny dip." His eyes twinkling, laughing at me again. He took my hand in his and brought my palm to his lips. His breath was warm and moist. I wanted him to kiss me, but he let go of my hand abruptly. "Wouldn't want to lose my head, Gitrhawn," he said and laughed.

I pushed him so that he almost lost his balance and fell into the water. But he grabbed onto my arm and held fast. Then he stood, pulling me up with him, and circled his arm around my waist. "It would almost be worth it," he said, his eyes unflinching. "But we don't belong in legends." He released me abruptly, strode to the fire, removed the sticks, and began to cover the ashes with sand. I waited by the water's edge.

Neither of us said anything while we climbed back into the boat. I took out my notebook and started writing some of what had happened. I didn't trust my voice or feelings. While I was scribbling, I was waiting for him to say something first.

Finally he said, "I really wanted you back there . . ."

"Let's not talk about it," I said quickly, contradicting my thoughts.

"It's not going to go away."

"Maybe not. But it's not going to happen either." I didn't look at him as I spoke and forced myself to think of Marc, waiting for me at home. I've hardly thought of him the whole time I've been away.

When we arrived back at the dock, I excused myself and went to the shed to hunt for Lila's notes, if they'd been kept. It gave me an excuse to think about something other than David. I suppose he sensed my withdrawal because he didn't follow me and we spent the rest of the day apart.

I found a small notebook with a silk Chinese cover. The flowers were faded and stained with dampness but the writing was still legible. I took the notebook up to my room to read in private.

Lila's Diary Entry #1

I ain't much good at writing down my thoughts, but I promised Miss Catherine to do this and I aim to keep my promise. It's just Sarah, Rhppeesunt, and me now living in this house. I got too much on my mind to worry about anybody. Got to care for Sarah. Got her a wet nurse for now, Rhppeesunt, though Miss Catherine calls her "Ruth." Her two-year-old don't need milk no more. Miss Catherine was real lucky to find her. She'll be around until Sarah can eat on her own.

I been real worried about Miss Catherine. I didn't want her going back by herself. But she says, "It's all right, Lila. You've got to take care of Sarah now." Poor little soul. I'll do my best by her, just like Miss Catherine wants.

I wish I could have stopped everything before it come to this. Nathaniel, he should have done it himself, and he would, if he'd been of the old tradition. But he been living around white men too long.

Miss Catherine, she give me this book just before we come out to the island and she says for me to write down everything that's happening to us. I think to myself, she wants me to learn better English, but she says she don't want to read it, it's to be my private book. But she asks me now and then if I been writing in it. So I tell her yes and there's plenty here about her too.

Two years ago, when we was still in Victoria, she got it in her head to go up and join Mr. Philip, he being so happy in Prince Rupert and all. I told her things aren't easy up north. Not like the city. I didn't want her to go. But she don't listen to nobody. She just makes up her mind to do something and then does it. So she decides I was going with her. Can't say I really minded in the end. She was a sister to me and I don't have no other family but my people up the Nass. They wouldn't have been too happy to see me. Too many things different. And me too. I was different. And I guess it was because of her.

Lila's Diary Entry #2

Miss Catherine, what she really wants me to do is write down all this so Sarah can find out about her one day. But she don't want Sarah to know until after she's gone. I been writing down what I know about what happened. And Miss Catherine made me promise to tell Sarah about her heritage. I been passing on old stories I heard from my own mother. Sarah's going to be proud of being Indian because if the white man had his way, we'd forget who we are. The missionaries don't like our ways neither. They want us to learn all about the white God. And I ain't blaming them for believing in something. We got our beliefs and they got theirs. Only they don't want ours to be passed on. They figure someone's got to be right and they're the ones that are. They say we got to get married in their churches, else we all go to Hell. I don't think there's a Hell like the way they tell it. But there's evil spirits that got to be reckoned with. But we do it our own way and pretend to believe what they tell us.

Lila's Diary Entry #3

It was my fault they met. Nathaniel, he comes from my village, back on the Nass River. Ran away when he was a boy, though he was twenty-four when we met up again. He was working at the railway company where Mr. Philip works. I saw him one day on the street, and we talked a bit. "I been back to the village," he says to me. I wanted to know about my family, so I says to Miss Catherine when I got home, "Could I invite him to the house some afternoon to talk to him?" And she says, "Of course, Lila. Anytime." But when he come, she don't let us just sit on the back porch and talk. She says, "You come on into the sitting room." Then she leaves us alone but not till after I introduce them. She liked him right away, I could see that, and he liked her. And when he went walking down the boardwalk, she come running out to the porch and asked him to come back again. I asked her, why did you do that for? And she says she wanted to hear all about my village. So, Nathaniel starts coming to the house a couple of times a week. At first, Miss Catherine sits quiet like and listens. She was always doing embroidery since we come up to Prince Rupert because she didn't like her hands being still. After a few weeks of this, I notices that she looks forward to his visits more than she tries to let on. Nathaniel never come when Mr. Philip was home. He was traveling again. The dock was all done and what, with the railway coming west from Winnipeg, Mr. Philip was always moving around, having to go and supervise something or other. Miss Catherine, she was alone most times, except for me. So, after a bit, she starts finding things for me to do when Nathaniel come. She sends me off on errands. I saw what was starting to happen. A couple of times I tries to bring it up with her, but she won't hear me talk about it. One time, I got hold of Nathaniel and told him he's got to stay away from her. But he says, "T'ain't your business, Lila." They was real careful. If anybody saw him coming to the house, Miss Catherine, she says he come calling on me. I didn't say nothing. If they was bent on falling in love, there was nothing I could do about it.

Lila's Diary Entry #4

At first, I pretend I don't hear her getting up at night and going out. I don't want to say nothin to her about it. I know he come for her somewhere out in the woods. I don't know where they go. One time, I was up when she come down with her cloak on. We was almost the same age, but she was like a young'un, all smiling and happy. She hugged me quick and said, "I love him. Be happy for me." No way I could fight that.

One day, she got this idea of building a house out on this island. She wrote Mr. Philip about it, like she wanted somewhere to go in the summers. He don't argue with her about nothing. He knows when she makes up her mind to have something, she gets it no matter what. So the builders come and in a few weeks, we got this house.

Mr. Philip come home unexpected like. Just before we was to move out. He sees the cases all packed and starts shouting at Miss Catherine.

"When you said a summer home, I thought you meant somewhere to spend a week or two for a vacation. *Together.*" He starts pacing around the trunks in the hallway. "I won't have you alone in the middle of nowhere. It's not safe."

I went into the kitchen but I could still hear them. Miss Catherine was sitting on the couch, embroidering, like nothing was wrong. She says to him she thought he wants her to be happy, he's always saying so. And he knows she don't like Prince Rupert. She's going to plant a vegetable garden on the island.

Then Mr. Philip says to her she's got no right to be deciding things without asking him. And she says he's always traveling and he never asks her what she wants.

"We're going over for the summer and you're not going to stop us," she says, and I hear her coming into the hall.

Then, Mr. Philip, he shouts, "All right. Who is it?"

And I get real anxious, like maybe he's heard something. But Miss Catherine, she says real calm like, "Who is who?"

"There's someone else, isn't there?" Mr. Philip says. "While I'm out there working to keep you happy, you're . . ."

"I-just-want-to-go-away-for-the-summer," Miss Catherine says real slow. "It's common practice in England. Why are you so upset?"

"We're not in England!" Mr. Philip says.

Then I hear Miss Catherine go up the stairs, like she's finished talking about it.

We didn't go right away, but Miss Catherine never unpacked the cases in the hall. We just walked around them. That night, she whispers to me, "Go tell Nathaniel that Mr. Philip's home."

The way things turned out, a bit of luck come our way. Near the end of the second week he's home, Mr. Philip gets a wire saying he has to go back to Winnipeg. Miss Catherine, she's real sweet, she says she's sad to see him go and, as soon as he's gone, we pack the rest of the things to go to the island and she finds a barge to ship her piano across.

It was the middle of May. Still a bit chilly on the water. On the way over, Miss Catherine says to me she's going to have Nathaniel's baby. "You've got to help with the delivery, Lila," she says. "You've been through it once already."

Lila's Diary Entry #5

Miss Catherine, she says to me, "Lila, if I get through this all right, I promise I'll go back to Mr. Philip and make it up to him." But I don't think she really believed it herself.

We was living in the house. Miss Catherine brought material and cushions and, for a while, we was busy sewing up things to make the house pretty. Nathaniel come on the weekends and I went out, so's I could leave them alone. I spent a lot of time worrying that somebody would come and find him there. We kept all to ourselves, she, Nathaniel, and me. We didn't want no one to know she was pregnant. The piano had come — it was something she couldn't live without, music. She played most nights while I sat near the fire knitting for the baby. Nathaniel was crazy for her. He always come with little presents. But she don't like store-bought things, so he made her things with his hands. Like toys out of wood, and necklaces for her made of pits and whalebone. One day, he comes with a bentwood box that he's made himself. It's all carved with birds, fish, people. When he gives it to her, he looks so sad, I know right away he's not coming back. Maybe she knows it too but don't ask. Nathaniel, he hasn't carved the box himself, he's taken it to our village and got it done by our best carver. There is a legend goes with it, and Nathaniel told it to Miss Catherine.

Lila's Diary Entry #6

We never saw Nathaniel after that time when he come with the box. Miss Catherine and me, we don't talk about it, like we was both of us afraid.

Miss Catherine, she's always sitting by the window looking at the dock, and stroking the box on her lap. And she tells me the legend over and over, like I never heard it before.

And a lot of nights, I wake up and find her standing on the dock, not even a shawl on her, and I think she'll surely catch cold, or maybe worse. She went on waiting for Nathaniel but he never come back. It wasn't too long after Sarah come, then a month passes and Miss Catherine's getting ready to go back.

And the day before she leaves, she says to me, "Sarah should have the box because it belongs to her father." But she took it with her when she left.

Porcher Island, July 16.

Last night, when I turned the page after Lila's sixth entry, I found next to the sewn binding, the jagged remains of six torn-out pages. I resolved to go back to the shed and search every box, although it occurred to me that whoever ripped out the pages may also have destroyed them.

Today, after lunch, David and I went out in the boat — guarded and distant. We avoid each other's eyes because there are too many needs in them; too many things we won't discuss. It is the ninth day. He has taken to calling me "Gitrhawn."

David rowed lazy under the hot sun. I lay in the bottom of the boat, notebook resting on my stomach. My sunglasses tinted the hazy smoky air with a soft purple hue. How easily perceptions are altered. I closed my eyes.

David said, "Hey. You're not supposed to fall asleep."

I smiled and relaxed into the lull of the waves.

"What, no story today?" he asked.

"None."

David stopped rowing. "Come on, you can make up something." His eyes twinkled.

"All right. Let me think for a minute." I closed my eyes again. I felt a little like Sheharazade. Will we end when my tale ends?

I told him about Lila's diary and, when I finished, we both lay at either ends of the boat, oars in. We'd been floating for a while. Now and then, when we got too close to shore, David rowed us back out. Porcher Island. A constant magnetic pull. Boats, canoes, all washed up on the same shore.

"But why did she go back to Philip?" David asked.

"Because she was vulnerable. Because he needed her. Because she was tired of waiting. Because it was better to have someone, even if he wasn't the one she wanted. I don't know. Probably all of this."

The sun burned, and I felt sticky with heat. David slid deeper into the bottom of the boat, the length of his left leg settling against my right one. I forced myself to ignore the new intimacy and stared overhead at the haze of smoke that hung like a thin cloud layer across the sky. Heat. Inside and out. He began to stroke my legs, pressing himself closer.

"Will the fires never stop?" I said. "All that timber burning. God it's hot." I shifted myself away from him and sat up.

"Gitrhawn. Gitrhawn." He murmured the name and brought his arms up under his head.

I pushed the sunglasses up into my hair and squinted at David.

He'd taken off his shirt while I talked and one of his fingers played circles on the skin behind my knees. I struggled to a sitting position. "I'm going for a swim." I slipped off my shirt and dove into the cool black water, leaving him to watch me from the boat.

At the end of my swim, when I tried to climb back inside, he held me off, peeled my fingers off the edge of the boat, one by one, until I fell back into the water. I managed finally to pull him in and while he splashed around, I quickly grabbed the sides and hauled myself into the boat. Then I tried to paddle away, laughing as he swam long strokes beside me.

"I'll get you for this," he said. "You'll be sorry."

He swam better than I rowed and caught up easily, pulling himself up in one quick motion. He sat across from me, dripping water onto my feet, took the oars and pushed them to one side.

"We better go back," I said. "It's almost dinner time."

"Not yet." He smiled. "Let's dry in the sun."

We lay back down, only this time he lay beside me, slipped his arm under my neck. "To make room for both our shoulders," he explained. I closed my eyes and leaned my head against his shoulder. We lay still and quiet and even now I don't know when we began to caress each other or even who started it. The heat drenched us. Sun caught in his fingertips. My own hands filled with his warmth. Our bodies oiled with perspiration, gliding, slippery, one against the other.

Night. Water splashes against the dock. I try not to think of David in the next room. A knot tightens in my abdomen — tells me that I'm not made for simple love affairs. I close my eyes and think of Marc, trying to remember some special moment. Before we moved in together, he said, "Why don't we get married?" And I said, "Why don't we just live together first?" I wasn't sure of us then and I'm even more unsure now. But I am comfortable with him. There are no knots, no doubts. I must tell David tomorrow.

The night is hot and humid. The moon's fingers trail across my bed. Then the door opens, forces the curtain to suck in its breath. David slips into bed beside me and the waiting stops.

❖

Porcher Island, February 7, 1987.

How foolish man is when it comes to love. And what is this elusive thing that makes us crave the touch of another's body; the need for two people to become one? Intimacy. Back to this word and its perfidious consequences.

I am tired of thinking. There is nothing left of what I once believed. There is no past and there is no future. I sit in this chair, motionless as the dock. We are both things that exist at this moment. The earth revolves, the tide comes in, goes out, the moon fulfills its cycles. These are eternal, predestined things. I have no course to follow. The things that happened in these pages, happened to someone else. I no longer believe the words. They have become a fiction. No past and no future. I am so tired.

✧

Porcher Island, July 17.

Sarah is napping by the window. David and Pearl have gone to Prince Rupert. I wonder if he'll phone her. His wife. The word sounds alien. He's never said it.

I feel restless, anxious. As if by contacting that other world, he is somehow betraying me. It's ridiculous to feel this way, I know, but I can't help thinking about yesterday. In the boat. In the silence of night. We've been distant to each other since then; regaining our equilibrium. Before they went this morning, I left my coffee cup half-full and ran upstairs to write Marc a letter. So that David would have to mail it. So that he'd know that nothing's changed. I'd brought several cards with me to send to Marc, just in case I missed him.

I felt hypocritical, silly, filling in the card. A card that said, "I Miss You," on the cover, hot pink letters on a black background. I couldn't think of anything to write on the inside and finally just scribbled my name.

Downstairs, David took the envelope and read the name and address. Pearl called from the living room that she was ready, and David put the envelope into his shirt pocket. I watched him stand, drain his coffee cup, and put it in the sink with slow and deliberate movements. When he reached the doorway, he turned to me. "It won't work, you know," he said. "Rattling chains. I don't believe in monsters." He left before I could think of anything to reply.

Sarah is awake. I'll write later.

David came in after wiping his feet noisily on the doormat, as if he wanted to be noticed. He carried his shirt and I couldn't help staring at his bare chest. He laughed at me and threw the shirt over his back, sleeves dangling in front. Then he came and sat beside me so close I could smell his sweat.

He stroked my arm lightly. "Had a good day?" he asked. "Got anything in that notebook I should see?"

I nodded, shook my head, and slammed the notebook shut. "How about you? Did you get everything done?" It sounded like an accusation, and I wondered if he knew I was referring to the phone call I thought he'd probably made.

"I mailed your letter, if that's what you're asking."

Later, David and I ate dinner outside on the porch, in the shade, plates balanced on our knees. Even this late, the sun was still hot and I felt small rivulets of sweat rolling down the inside of my arm. We decided to go for a swim and I went upstairs to change. Then we dove off the dock while Sarah watched.

We surfaced on the other side, the one Sarah couldn't see, and treaded water, one hand clinging to the dock.

"I missed you today," David whispered, as if someone could hear him.

I moved a little away from him. "No you didn't at all." I smiled, pleased.

"Yes I did," he insisted, then added, "but only because you're the only pretty thing here."

I pouted, playful.

"Only teasing. The last part, I mean. I really did miss you."

"I suppose you have women in every port," I said lightly. "Or should I say, on every dock?"

His answer was serious. "Only one commitment. But when I'm away . . ."

I listened to the unspoken words, then said, "I've always been monogamous," in a tone I instantly thought sounded stuffy and judgemental.

"So, what's happened here?"

I felt like a child caught in a lie. I splashed water in his face and dunked him, but he pulled me down with him and kissed me underwater. I fought him off and surfaced, my hand grasping the dock. He kept his arm around my waist.

"I'm afraid," I said.

"Of me?" He smiled.

"No — yes." I wanted to tell him that I was afraid *for* me. "Couldn't we just be good friends?" I said.

He stared hard at me for a moment. "I thought that's what we were," he said finally.

Later, it was too hot to stay indoors. We found some old deck loungers in the shed and settled into them by the side of the house. There was no breeze to fan the branches of the trees overhead. Even the birds were silent, exhausted. We watched the sun rust the sky, then fall lazy into the sea. I could see the boat bob against the dock and, above the metal engine, heat spiralled like colorless smoke, distorting the sea behind it. I shut my eyes and dozed for a bit. When I next opened them, dusk had crept all around us. David was watching me.

"Tired?" he said softly.

I nodded. He'd tiptoed out of my room after dawn. We'd only slept a few hours.

"Feel like talking?"

I wasn't sure what he meant by this, so I shook my head. He stared at me for a moment, and I thought he was going to say something, but he only murmured, "Gitrhawn."

This evening, I felt his distance. I don't want us to be just good friends. There are only two days left. I want to touch him. I want us to become a legend, an indelible romantic tale told and retold in generations to come. Instead, I classify things tidily and conveniently. Control.

But he is obeying my rules. This evening, I missed his spontaneous gestures — the arm around my shoulders, his fingers on the inside of my elbow. You can't have it both ways, I told myself. Decisions. Patterns. Cycles. Lying in bed at night, trying to unravel my words, like Penelope. Avoiding the end. I didn't mean it. I did mean it. If I could erase these pages and begin each as page one, I would.

In the darkness, I watch tree shadows web the ceiling. Raven spirits watching over me, over David in the next room. Only two days left. Right time, wrong place. Right place, wrong time. We're out of synch. Haven't I been in love a dozen times? Is this any different? I can't remember. Selective memory. David says the things I want to hear, as if he's reading from a play I've written, a play we're both familiar with.

I get up and tiptoe into his room, into his warmth.

Porcher Island, July 18.

David didn't leave my side all morning. There is an urgency in both of us — as if we have something we want to say, but can find no words to express it. Sometimes, we both begin talking at once, then both fall silent. Perhaps I'm imagining that we want to say the same things. I must tell him my thoughts before I leave. Tomorrow. I'm finding it unbearable to be so close to him, but I would find it worse if he were not here. He is not mine yet he belongs to me. How will I ever leave this island

and its memories? We have been replaying the negative images of a passed-down legend. I see his face; the laughter of sun in his eyes; green seaweed and droplets of black water. This island. Has it been made of pebbles — memories — hurled on crests of waves to beat relentless against the dock? Has David only happened because I have willed it so? Am I telling and retelling my own story? Must I choose? These questions circle inside me, with no answers. I wonder if he is hearing them also.

A neighbor asked David to help him put up a new fence in the early afternoon. In exchange, later on, he'll lend us his truck. There's a lake and a waterfall, David told me, up a long dusty road.

I resumed my search of the shed while he was gone. Old clothes, music books, some children's clothing. I found one more letter from Philip to Catherine. Then, halfway down an old steamer trunk, I discovered what I was looking for. All six pages carefully laid into a blank notebook. Did Lila tear them out then save them? I took my treasure to my room, to add to the rest. Catherine's story, as complete as it can ever be. It's almost over. Tomorrow I leave. The twelfth day. David has said nothing about later.

Lila's Diary Entry #7

I didn't want to write this down before. In case Miss Catherine might see it. It's the only secret I ever had from her.

But now I know for sure she ain't never coming back, I want to put it down for Sarah.

It was the end of that first summer when we come out here. After Nathaniel brought the box for Miss Catherine. For days, she sits there, staring out at the dock, then, when he doesn't come for two weeks, she says, "Lila, you go across to get news." Her time was near and I didn't want to leave her but she says, "Lila, I've got to know what's happening." She been having nightmares, talking crazy. About legends she heard me and Nathaniel tell. "Woman-of-the-Woods. I saw her Lila. And she's got Nathaniel." And me there stroking her head, and sitting with her till she fall asleep again. But she wouldn't get no rest, not till I promised to go to Prince Rupert.

I got in the small boat. I was used to the ride; been going across about once a month or so all summer to get supplies and give Mr. Philip news.

At first, I went to the office of Grand Trunk Railway and asked about Nathaniel. I says, "He's my young man and I ain't seen him for a bit." The secretary, she looks in the book and tells me he don't work there. I ask, does she know why? But she says, "No. It just says 'terminated' and the date."

When I got back to the house, Mr. Philip was there. He says to me, "Lila, you've been to the office asking questions. Why didn't you come to me?" He looked cold and strange and I was afraid of him. I says to him what I says to the secretary, that I'm looking for my young man. He stares at me, hard, and says, "Stop it. I know what's been going on. He's back in his home, where he belongs. It's finished." Then he puts his hand on my arm and it's as cold as the side of a boat on a winter morning. "And don't you tell her a word about it," he says, "or I'll see to it she's finished along with that bastard child she's carrying." He lets go of me and walks to the door, then stops. From inside his jacket, he takes out a letter, all sealed up, and throws it on the window ledge. "See she gets that," he says, then turns and leaves.

I went out in the boat and sat there for a bit. I knew I couldn't go back and face Miss Catherine without knowing, so I decides to go to my village on the Nass. Then I could talk to Nathaniel, to see if he really was doing all right.

I kept close to shore. I hadn't been back home for years, not once since I left. I felt mixed-up about seeing my old home. Not knowing if it was changed or the same. I spent the time looking at the banks. Here and there, smoke curled up from behind the trees but I didn't know if these were new Indian or white settlements. Finally I come to the village and go right to the house of Klootsmah, an old woman who was my mother's friend. I ask her about Nathaniel. Klootsmah don't speak no English, or don't want to, but when I says "Nathaniel," she puts her finger in front of her lips. Then, she spits on the ground. "White men," she says.

So I begs her to tell me what's happened to him and she gets up and waves her arm for me to come. I follow Klootsmah up through the woods about a mile, till we gets to a small missionary church. She don't come no further but points past the log building to a plot with wooden crosses. "Buried him like a white man," she says and spits again before turning back. I went on up slowly to the freshly-dug grave. The earth was chocolate brown and heaped uneven like. I remember I got to thinking about our vegetable garden on the island, and how Miss Catherine wouldn't plant nothin' in flat ground. Nathaniel, he was always teasing her, saying her garden looked like a plot of fresh graves, she wanted the ridges so high.

There was a rough cross at one end — made of stripped tree branches — with his initials carved where the face of a Christian God would be. I remember it, and all the hurting inside and how I couldn't believe it. Nathaniel, sweet and gentle, him quiet and laughing, his love for Miss Catherine — all buried inside this strange and lonely place. I remember crying and falling on my knees and clawing at the earth, so's I could see him myself to believe. The Preacher and his wife, they must have heard me because they come running from the mission. For a bit, we's struggling on the grave, me screaming Nathaniel's name and the Preacher chanting some prayer over and over, willing the Devil away. The Preacher's wife, she slaps me hard on the face and I stop fighting. But I keeps on crying even after there's no tears left, rocking on my knees beside him, crying for me and Miss Catherine, because I knew I'd never tell her.

The Preacher's wife helped me up and says, "Come on inside for a hot drink of coffee." And I was glad she don't ask no questions as I followed her, hoping maybe she's got something to tell me.

"He your husband?" she asks when we's sitting at the kitchen table.

I nodded because it's easier.

"I'm sorry," she says.

"How'd he . . . ?"

"Found him in the bottom of a canoe. Someone must have pulled it and left it on the bank. Had a bullet in him. And he'd been beaten bad. The village folk said he was a bad omen. They didn't want no trouble."

"What about a doctor? Why didn't you take him to a doctor?"

"Too late. He come home to die." She pats my hand. "You called Catherine?"

So I nod again, numb.

"He said your name till the end. I thought you'd want to know. He was thinking about you right to the end."

Then I starts crying again and she sits across from me and starts reading out of her prayer book, her voice all one tone. Then she says, "You's welcome to spend the night. My husband can read a service in the morning."

But I shook my head and got up to leave. At the door I says to her, "This was never his home." Then I went on back through the woods to Klootsmah's house. For a long time I lay awake, trying to decide what to do, whether to tell her or not. When dawn came, I got in the boat and went back to the island.

October, 1910

Catherine,

Isn't it time you stopped hiding and came home?
I know it hasn't been easy for you with me away
most of the time these past few years. But all
that has changed. Let's put the past behind us.
There's so much to live for in the future.
I'll be overseeing the building of the new
drydocks here. I'm asking you to come home so we
can begin a real family life together.

Philip

Catherine had underlined the words, *Let's put the past behind us*, and written at the bottom, *"What have you done with Nathaniel?"*

Porcher Island, July 19.

Morning. The last day. David and I sitting on the dock, feet swinging in the water. Everything packed, neatly folded in suitcases. After lunch, he was to take me across the water for the last time. He took my hand, moved closer.

I said, "Sarah will see us."

He didn't answer, just continued to hold my hand.

I knew what I was saying didn't really make sense. I was trying to say other things. "Aren't you worried? She might tell your . . ."

"Sarah knows."

I thought of plausible variations. Sarah knows I'm leaving; Sarah knows we're just friends; Sarah knows I don't want to leave; Sarah knows David will forget me as soon as I'm gone; Sarah knows we've fallen in love.

I liked the last one best. Is that what happened? I wanted to ask David how he felt. But he remained so guarded; so distant. We have been lovers. Will it all end for him when I step into that boat? For me? There can be no answers until later. After we've parted.

I gazed down at the water; made small whirlpools with my toes. He stroked my ankle with his foot underwater.

"She won't make it till Christmas," he said suddenly.

"What do you mean?" I asked, although I understood perfectly. I wanted him to say that it meant something else. I tried again to think of plausible variations. There weren't any. It was too specific. Too truthful. I'd known, but had purposely pushed it to the back of my mind, to keep it from surfacing. I'd found justifications for the signs — the thin, frail body, the pained expressions in the window, the click-click of needles marking off her days like the second hand on a watch — signs my subconscious could not ignore.

"Elise, I'm sorry," David said, calling me by my name for the first time since I'd arrived.

I turned to look at the window, at the old woman asleep, her head leaning on one shoulder.

"Can there not be one happy ending?" I said, tears stinging my eyes.

"I'm sorry," he repeated. "I thought you should know."

I walked quickly up the dock, away from that window and David. He didn't try to call me back. When I entered the woods, I left the path and began to run through dense underbrush. I clawed at branches, felt them snap back against my bare legs. Secrets, past, present, future — all opaque. I would lose them both. I lay down in the earth and cried.

A minute. An hour. Two? David walked towards me. He didn't say anything; simply lay beside me, took me in his arms, and held me. I shut my eyes against the curve of his neck.

He put his hand under my chin, raised my head to look at him. "Gitrhawn?" he murmured.

I pulled him down against me for a moment and his mouth brushed my forehead, my eyes, my cheeks. There was no time left. I slowly disengaged myself and sat up. Beside me lay a long dry branch with leaves still attached. I swept it in a semi-circle around my feet. Back and forth. Back and forth until there was nothing left but hard-packed dirt.

David stood and offered me his hand. "Come on. We'd better go back. You've got a plane to catch."

I let him pull me to my feet. We walked back in silence, hand-in-hand, fingers intertwined.

Later, in the boat going across the harbor, I kept biting my lip, swallowing the lump in my throat, to keep from crying. I waved to Sarah until we went around a point of land and I couldn't see the house any more. I tried to recall details, but already I couldn't remember. How many boats were there? Did they have names? All I could see was the old frail face at the window, blue eyes and a white hanky.

He took me directly to Dighby Island, bypassed Prince Rupert. He couldn't moor there for long. Perhaps he chose this way so he could avoid a lengthy farewell.

After he'd put my bag on the bus to the airport, I walked back with him to the boat.

He said, "I hate goodbyes."

"Yes."

We stood, awkward, then I moved to embrace him but he held me away from him. "I'll let you know about Sarah," he said, then turned and stepped into the boat.

The bus driver honked and, for a moment, I thought of

leaving everything, of stepping into the boat with David, of living forever on Porcher Island. The boat's engine coughed, then roared to life. The bus's horn, insistent. David, his back to me, untied the boat. My cheeks were wet and I started towards the bus, stumbling backwards, waiting for David to turn, to speak, to do something that could change this moment.

The boat began to move away from the dock. The bus covered the distance between us and I stepped inside. I stood in the stepwell and watched until finally David turned and raised his hand in farewell.

PREMISE:
*The Case
Studies*

"I've got her first name," Paul tells Annie on the phone on Sunday afternoon. "And a man's name. The father likely."

"Paul, where have you been? I thought you went fishing."

"I did go fishing. I went fishing on Porcher Island. If you could see the place, Annie. And all the stuff she's written. I just hope she's all right."

"Trying to kill her baby does not exactly make her all right."

"It's not like that," Paul says. "There's the legend and all the things that came before. She thinks she's fulfilling some kind of cycle."

"A sick cycle, if you ask me."

"You just don't understand yet."

"Suppose you explain it to me. You want to come over?"

"All right. In a while." After he hangs up, Paul showers, then goes to his office and makes a copy of the manuscript. He returns to his apartment and leaves the original there before he goes to Annie's house.

He and Annie sit on her sun porch until dusk. Then they move inside. Paul re-reads each page after Annie has finished. At the end, she sits quiet, staring at the table.

"Well? What do you think?" Paul asks.

"I'm not sure. She's obviously distraught. But what do you think really happened out there with that man?"

Paul shrugs. "I suppose he got her pregnant." Then he adds, "Though I don't think he intended to."

"Do you think he knows?"

"No idea. I'll give him a call tomorrow. Lives in Winnipeg. We'll ask him."

"What about the boyfriend she was living with? Marc."

"We're not going to find him without a last name. But maybe David Williams will help. He must have her address. We'll trace it."

When he gets home, Paul flips through the original pages until he finds the recent entries. February. Three months ago.

Intimacy. Her words have struck a harmonious tone in him. He thinks perhaps this is why he's never married. He's had relationships. Two, three year affairs. Nothing permanent. He wonders if she's right. If two people are destined to always remain separate individuals; if intimacy is an abstraction which comes into focus now and then, unexpected as a hail storm in summer. Perhaps, like her, he simply wills it not to happen. His will motivated by fear. Yes, he admits, he is afraid to allow someone to come so close to him.

"I had no idea," David Williams says, putting the diary down on the table in Paul's hotel room.

Paul watches him from an easy chair. He thinks David looks embarrassed, uncomfortable. "Is it true?" he asks.

"We — had a brief affair, if that's what you're asking," David answers, hesitant.

Paul taps his pen against the diary. "But was that all there was to it? Just a brief affair?"

David shifts in the chair and Paul wishes he didn't have to ask these questions. Some things are too personal to verbalize. He waits patiently for David to speak.

"I really did care for her. But — well, I'm a married man. She knew that. And she was living with someone also." David runs a hand through his hair. "I'm not saying I didn't feel the same as she did, it's just that, well — when you get to be this age, you weigh things. Priorities. All of that. It's not like being nineteen. You can't change partners so easily any more." He pauses and flips through the right-hand corner of the manuscript, like a deck of cards. "Perhaps it's the realization that in the end, it would all be the same anyway. After a while, you'd settle into a comfortable relationship. And I already had that. Can you understand what I mean?"

Paul nods. "Perhaps this was the real difference between you," he says to David. "I don't think the young woman was settled in a comfortable relationship. Or if she was, she didn't appear to enjoy it."

"I thought we were quite similar," David says. "Certainly in that we thought in the same way. And when we met, we — *recognized* each other, if that's possible. Recognized something about our personalities, characters, whatever. But I thought she understood my situation better than she did."

"You had no idea she was pregnant," Paul states quietly.

"No. But now I realize that she probably tried to tell me."

"Did you correspond with her?" Paul is surprised.

"I wrote to her when Sarah died. Thought she'd want to know or perhaps come to the funeral."

"And did she? When was that?"

"In late November of last year. No, she didn't come, but she wrote to say that it was most important for me to meet her in Vancouver after the funeral and go with her to Barkerville."

Paul sighs. So it was the two of them there. "What happened?"

"It was very strange. We went up, got a motel room in Wells. That's the closest accommodation you can get to Barkerville. But we didn't" — David looks up, embarrassed — "sleep together. The next morning, we drove to Barkerville. There was a lot of snow and we couldn't get skis, so we ended up walking around a little on the cleared paths." David pauses. "I suppose she wanted to tell me about the baby. When we got back to Wells in the afternoon, I laid down for a nap. She was gone when I woke up."

"Gone?"

"I haven't seen her since. She left me the car. Must have hitched a ride back to Quesnel."

"Didn't you try to contact her?" Paul asks.

"No. I thought it best to let things be." David shakes his head. "I had no idea."

195

Paul swivels in small half-arcs in his chair. "Do you have any idea where she might be?"

"No. I have her address, the one she gave me last summer. But the fellow she was with, Marc Kohn was his name, he might know."

"Just as a matter of interest, what do you think about the legend?" Paul asks.

David shrugs. "It's as she told it in the diary. I didn't believe her legend. She made it up. Although why she did that, I have no idea." He strokes the top page of the diary, smoothing the corners. "What will happen to the baby?" he asks.

Paul is startled, he didn't expect this question. "She'll be put up for adoption," he says quietly.

"You understand my position," David says. "I mean, there's no way to prove she really is my daughter. Although," he adds quickly, "if that were the case — if Elise said so — I would certainly take the financial responsibility."

"I understand," Paul says. "I'll keep in touch if anything new develops."

Deposition Given June 21, 1987
by Marc Leslie Kohn
to Detective Paul Evans

EVANS: For the record, I'm going to ask you to report some things you've already told me.
KOHN: Fine.
EVANS: Your full name?
KOHN: Marc Leslie Kohn.
EVANS: Occupation?
KOHN: Research Assistant.
EVANS: Address?
KOHN: 5243 West 6th Avenue, Vancouver.
EVANS: The full name of the young lady you co-habited with?
KOHN: Elise Slayte.
EVANS: Her occupation?
KOHN: She didn't work. She had some money left her when her parents died. It was enough for her to live on the interest, so she didn't have to work. Closest thing to an occupation, I'd say, would be a professional student. She was always at the university. Read a lot; spent most of her time reading. And she kept diaries and I don't know what else. She wouldn't . . . she never showed me any of it. She was in her study all the time. Sometimes, she'd get up in the night and go write. She never asked me to read any of it.
EVANS: How long have you known Miss Slayte?
KOHN: Well . . . let me see . . . we moved in together in the spring of 86. April or May, I think it was. But I'd known her for a while. We'd been going together off and on for about three years before that.
EVANS: As you know, April last, a baby was found abandoned in a canoe. We have reason to believe Miss Slayte was the

mother. Did you know she was pregnant?

KOHN: Of course not. And I can hardly believe that it was her anyway. She's not the type of person who would just get pregnant. She'd have to plan it. She's very careful. Very aware. I can't believe that in her state of mind she'd get pregnant. It's just not like Elise.

EVANS: How would you describe her state of mind?

KOHN: Elise was not very stable. *She* knew she wasn't stable. *I* knew she wasn't. It was just the way she was. And right after we moved in together, things began to change.

EVANS: How did they begin to change?

KOHN: Well, she started going away a little bit at a time. At first, she went off for maybe a day or two. Went to visit a friend, or at least that's what she told me. I never asked. She was that kind of person. You didn't . . . you didn't *ask* where she was going. You didn't think she'd want to tell you and she wouldn't want you to ask, in any case. I thought it all extremely unhealthy. This was a new phase we hadn't gone through, but then, we hadn't lived together before. So I assumed she simply needed more room. She's a very distant person. Always kept herself very separate from me. From everyone. And I knew if I tried to get too close to her, that'd be the end of it. So I just let her have lots of room. Didn't crowd her ever. I knew she'd always come back because she needed me in her own way.

EVANS: I understand last summer she was on Porcher Island for about two weeks.

KOHN: Yes. That was the longest she was away. Sent me a couple of postcards. Said she was all right. Other than that, I had no idea . . . I assumed she was in Prince Rupert because of the postmarks. But she never indicated when she was coming back or anything. As I stated earlier, however, I didn't worry about her. She was still keeping contact with me.

EVANS: What you're saying is you had an unspoken arrangement?

KOHN: Of a kind. I would have liked a more . . . one time I

asked her to marry me and she absolutely refused. She said she wasn't made for permanent things. That's why I really think there's no way that she would even consider having a child. I'm sure of it. I knew her *that* well.

EVANS: Did anything happen when she returned from her trip? Anything different?

KOHN: Not really. Whatever happened, happened while she was away. She got back . . . oh . . . mid or late July, I think. And she was more distant than ever. Usually, after being gone, she settled down for a while. But not this time. She spent most of her time in the study . . . middle of the night . . . would hardly talk to me for days.

EVANS: Did you try to discuss this with her?

KOHN: As I've tried to explain, she wasn't the type of person you could discuss something like this with. Very intense. When there was something wrong, you just let it ride and eventually it would go away. But when she came back that time, well . . . I knew it had gone too far. It was inevitable that she was going to leave.

EVANS: I've found some manuscripts. Are you familiar enough with her handwriting to identify it?

KOHN: Of course. She might not have let me see what she was writing, but I certainly know her handwriting.

EVANS: Tell me, in your opinion, if this is hers.

KOHN: Yes, of course. It's Elise's writing. Where did you get these?

EVANS: In a house on Porcher Island. She must have kept the diary while she was there.

KOHN: Well — I've seen some of this — I think part of it, at least, was written here when she came back. When she was in Vancouver. Before she left. Yes, I'm sure of it. I'm sure I've seen this before.

EVANS: But I thought you said you never read what she wrote.

KOHN: I said she never *showed* me what she wrote. But when

things got real bad . . . sometimes I'd go into her study when she wasn't there, and just look through and see . . . just read through some of the stuff she was writing to see if I could . . . understand what was going on. And when I came across these pages, I realized that she'd met somebody else up north and so I . . . I just thought there was no point . . . in me questioning her about it. If she didn't want to tell me about it, there was no point asking her.

EVANS: Could she have left them there for you to read?

KOHN: Oh no. She would have been furious. She had this thing about privacy. And I respected it, for the most part.

EVANS: When did you see her last?

KOHN: Last November. I came home one day and all her things were gone. No explanations. No goodbyes. It was as if she'd never been there. She left me one thing — a poem. I assume it was written to me, although none of the things she wrote that I said or did are true.

EVANS: May I see it?

KOHN: Sure. I'll get it.

EVANS: Would it be all right if I were to make a copy of this?

KOHN: Sure. I don't see how it's going to help find her, though.

EVANS: Is there any place you can think of where she may have gone?

KOHN: Like I said earlier, she went away a lot. Never said where, specifically.

EVANS: I'll leave my card. In case you hear from her. Thank you for your time.

POEM FROM ELISE

Intimate Partners

We lie face to face
between pages of a magazine.
Years have rendered us mute, gestures
cryptic and rhetorical. We fit snug into habits,
cloistered.
Experts use terms like
"dysfunctional rules of the relationship," and
"polarize,"
as if we were abstractions,
beams of a northern light
shooting into each other
the reflection of a crystalline frost.

They have reduced us to clichés;
I see myself too clearly, and you too.
So I ask you, my love,
while stroking the soft flesh, your inner thigh,
I ask, this intimacy thing,
you and I, what do you make of it?
wondering in my head
why we don't say the words.
You tell me actions speak
that what I read
are fabricated aberrations
these experts, you say, need a disease
in order to effect a cure.
Your arm circles my waist
fingers calm on the spine.

You will enter me with those hands
if I let you
you will force the blades apart
and draw out the Chimaera,
flames torching the flesh, my lion's mouth
the goat body
the serpent's tail lashing.
But you have no leaden spears, my Bellerophon,
you have only a mouth without words
and a hard male body thrusting blind
against me.

I distance you with a turn of the head.
You will never know
what's inside the dark mouth of the cave
or how close you sometimes come to those passages;
I feel you trembling at the entrance
and slam the door just in time.
Do you want to know me, my love?
What can I tell you that you'll believe?
I will listen to the experts, take their advice.
Listen, my love, listen and don't reply. I will tell you

there is no present. You and I are a story
I'll recount one day
to a group of women laughing in a smoke-filled bar
pouring liquor into the hole in their hearts.
I will make us a sentimental tale, perhaps,
filled with regrets and the perception of time;
or I will reduce this moment to a skit,
tell how we never could synchronize our signals,
how we bounced off each other like magnets and lay sprawled
on the sheets of a king-sized bed
a continent between us.

I reach across the distance for your hand. Listen, my love
to the ticking in my heart
measuring out time as if it were a finite thing.
I will kill you in the end,
it's so ordained. You've given me
the tablet inscribed with deadly signs.
I run my fingers across the trust in your eyes
you are blind and languish in your own reflection;
this night will end.

Your crimson ray reaches my mouth. Listen, my love,
and don't reply to the rising rhythm within me
to the fanned embers of a familiar fire.
I will recount this too
at a kitchen table, among women who shed men
like debris,
who stuff laughter into the seams in their hearts.
I will tell you were a sword of bronze
too near the mouth,
how my lips turned to flames

how you melted drop by drop onto the white sheets.
You stir between my thighs. Listen, my love,
to the pulse of this myopic moment. Tomorrow
we will be adversaries. But for tonight, we are one,
intimate partners.
I lie against you
your hair, the strings of a harp lulling sleep
your even breath, sweet as Orpheus's song:

Come from the cloudy west
Soft over brain and breast
Bidding the Dragon rest,
  Come to me, Sleep!

the coils soften, uncurl
for tonight, I will let you reach through the bars
of my ribcage to touch my fragile dreams:

> I am Athene, eyes flashing
> I have only to bind my feet with sandals
> of untarnishable gold
> to rise above the collective sigh
> of women pacing a treadmill of mistakes,
> bound between pages of history,
> of social injustices;
> I can forget myself, my sex, and find
> in the layer of a cloud
> a male head, a tongue which speaks truth,
> a body not yet born;

> I am Calypso
> lying in the scent of cypress
> in the fragrance of cleft cedar blazing
> and sandal wood, pouring nectar
> over the shoulders of an intrepid man
> who says, I love you, with conviction
> who braids his destiny with mine
> and does not weep on the shores of his past;

> I am Penthesilea,
> on the banks of the river Thermodon
> flanked by all women; we daughters of the God of War
> avenged,

powerful,
without longing for a male body
a river of semen
a perfidious tongue gutting the soul.

At first light, I stir, open my eyes
and see the cavity laid bare;
you lie sleeping, slender flanks poised
as a knife. You could awaken now
plunge yourself to the hilt
and count the drops
blood seeping into my lungs,
you could stain me forever on these white sheets.

Slowly I pry your fists
from my ribs, use scar tissue
to mend the gaps. I curl into myself,
gather strength; you turn,
spoon around me.
I am tight as a porcupine
can you not feel, my love, the distance,
the scales tipping
my equilibrium regained;
don't come too close
these quills are ready,
razor sharp. One moment more
you strain against me
I rise, bristling, slip from between sheets,
hide my nakedness. I have slain men
who tried to possess me as you do now;
don't come too close, my love.
Imagine for a moment this room, eternal night,
imagine this edge, the dark banks of the river Oceanus,

imagine grey spectres, phantoms of past lovers.
Another morning like this one, my love,
I will kill you on the edge of this bed
where you strip me in the name of love.

I don't understand you, you say, don't say,
a bitter edge to your silence. I want to hold you,
to tell you I don't understand myself,
that I heed an inner warning,
a whirlpool, Charybdis, narrowed between my breasts,
churning in time to a moon
spinning in perpetual motion; if I could, my love,
I would pluck out that golden coin
and with it, buy the solace of eternal peace.
You stare at me, your brows are dark
and furled,
you say I thrive on this razor's edge,
when too comfortable, I sharpen the blade.
I spend the day alone; read
what the experts say about us,
intimacy,
power struggles,
emotional systems.
I do the tasks:
"effective strategems for initiating change."

Task 1: Talking and Listening

I must speak only of myself. Not you. Not us.
Will you listen, my love, and not reply?
I will tell you
how I began to follow the footsteps of my father, Ulysses,
how my mother was not like other women,
how I blossomed in a confusion of flight
knowing departures
would bring the ecstacy of returns.

I will tell you of my first love at sixteen
spilling over the edge of a glacial lake, black water,
and he, twice my age
kept to the shallow end. We were not lovers
father and daughter treading nude
in that liquid innocence and sensuality.
He will remain forever an illusion
I created on the brink of womanhood.
You watch me, question with your eyes.
Don't speak, my love.
It does not matter how or when

it ended. But I will tell you. It was a letter
I sent after wedding vows to a man
young and slim, beautiful as Achilles;
a man with the gentle countenance of maidens;
a man I could clothe in armor and urge to battle,
brandishing ashen spears. You smile, my love,
I have turned him into myth;
such happens with retelling.
The truth now: he was safe, bound to my wishes
and would not depart

even later, when I begged freedom and fled
across a continent.

I need not tell you more. These two
are all the men I've loved; an alternating pattern
an odyssey
"autonomy and intimacy," the experts label my needs,
these serial monogamies. You have not heard a word
and think I fester this disease
and do not want a cure.
I am a dreamer inside a dream
sucking lotus-plants
to dull the ache of memories —
all of us made of glass
no diamond can cut.

Task 2: Odd Day, Even Day

These experts, ever-classifying, call me a "distancer"
in headlong flight; suggest I take odd days
and make one intimate request.
What will I ask of you, my love? On the beach,
we walk the sand of a low tide the moon has wrapped
around her wrists;
pursued by footprints, temporal as the present,
welts which will remain
until the moon loosens her bracelets,
casts them back to shore.
There is still time.
A train rounds the bend on serpentine tracks
nudging the curves of this bay, trailing a thousand ghosts

of strangers departing. Come, my love,
to the edge of those tracks,
lie with me on shards of blasted rock,
face inches from the steel.
Taste the elixir; we will become one. Can you hear
the weight collapsing our lungs? Hush, my love,
and watch those wheels,
heavy and rusted beside your eyes
while I whisper the crushing of bones
the severing of limbs. But you are mad, you say,
it's dangerous,
morbid. You distance me.
I distance you,
leave you to sink
in dry white sand, and climb the bank.

Task 3: Adding Requests

I am lost in these pages; among words foreign
as our needs. How can I ask more
of what you cannot give?
The experts know nothing
a mountain trail
a moraine of polished stone
and pools hollowed into the curves of a woman,
straticulated,
plunging into the earth's belly.
Walk with me, my love,
on the smooth hard flanks.
Above us, a dam bulges with the weight
of a glacier melting. Lie with me on the jagged edge,

arms flailing the abyss
and wait past the warning bells,
the open gates,
until we hear the roar,
see white foam swallow the stone. There will be time
to scramble onto land; a primal chaos
pumping adrenalin in the arteries.
The experts know nothing
the cloak of snow outside the window
the dead silencing of a heart. Come with me now
to the extremities; we'll drive a lonely road
and etch ourselves side by side in virgin snow.
Turn out the lights, my love,
let the moon spill in your eyes
and I will whisper that there are no edges
that these white shoulders are flimsy as mist
that your hands can only control
a body driven off the ends of its nerves.

Task 4: Control and Meta-Control

It has come to this: the experts' language consumed
in its own rhetoric.
Control.
We lie in the arc of twilight
day and night
swivelling on the axis of a phantom future.
You have not heard a word.
Who will you have me be tonight, my love,
you who need constant disguises? I reassure you
with my complicity; you forage me
while I leave you

to search a mountain stream
filled with the flowing robes
of my sisters, the Clouds,
where I can cleanse myself
laughing, until you drop a stone,
surprise me on the moss of a bank;
I don't recognize you, my love,
the dog's head drawn over your face,
bared canine teeth gnashing in a dream;
Asclepius says if you rob me of my clothes
I will be yours forever. You trap me
in the dark of a half-haloed moon, but I, Nephele,
cannot live without tears
and the melancholy of rain.

I turn the page, my tasks undone.
Outside the window, a black hole fills with grief
and the tortured sighs of lovers.
Will my odyssey never end?
I lie in the mouth of the river Phasis
and flow to the brink of a certitude,
an inevitable epilogue. Will you always,
stand aside
and watch my callisthenics, assured
that when exhausted,
you will lead me back to this bed,
to bleed onto white sheets?
One arid summer morning, I will kill you
with this edge
but for tonight, my love,
let us be intimate strangers.

❖

Dr. Magda Tremblay
P S Y C H I A T R I S T

July 4, 1987

Detective Paul Evans
RCMP Detachment
Prince Rupert, B.C.

Dear Detective Evans:

I am writing with regard to an investigation you are conducting concerning the identity of the woman who abandoned her baby last April, 1987. Under the law, I am obligated to act upon information given to me by a client, once I have formulated the opinion that said information is veritable and not a part of her delusional system.

Miss Elise Slayte was my client from April 27 to May 11, 1987. Please be advised that in the course of our discussions, she has imparted information which leads me to believe her to be the woman you are seeking.

                                                Sincerely yours,

                                                Dr. M. Tremblay

TRANSCRIPTS OF SUBPŒNAED TAPES
RECORDED BY DR. MAGDA TREMBLAY, PSYCHIATRIST,
BETWEEN APRIL 27, 1987 AND MAY 11, 1987.

TAPE #1: APRIL 27, 1987.

SLAYTE: I suppose you're wondering why I'm here. I mean, well, I don't look sick, do I?
DR. TREMBLAY: One's problems are not necessarily physically displayed.
SLAYTE: Exactly.
[*Pause*]
TREMBLAY: Do you want to talk about it?
SLAYTE: [*Sigh*] That's just it, you see. No one knows what goes on inside another person. Do you know the whole world is made up of liars, well, perhaps not liars, but — performers. People saying one thing and thinking another. As if we're all acting in a universal script. In Technicolor. Universal Studios. [*Laugh*] Always acting. You're acting right now.
TREMBLAY: Am I?
SLAYTE: Of course you are. Who isn't? Tell me that. Who isn't? The now and then I haven't been acting, no one believed my lines. Ironic, isn't it? We are trained from birth to say what other people want to hear.
TREMBLAY: And you? Are you acting now?
SLAYTE: [*Laughs*] Ah. Very clever. No, I needn't act with you. I don't know you.
TREMBLAY: Um?
SLAYTE: I mean, there's no point. It doesn't matter, you see, what strangers think about us. They're never going to get close to us.
TREMBLAY: I don't understand your logic. Shouldn't we be most

truthful with those who are close to us?
SLAYTE: Never. We'd only give them weapons.
[*Pause*]
SLAYTE: You see, I don't believe in intimacy.
TREMBLAY: And how would you define intimacy?
SLAYTE: I don't know. Letting someone absorb you. Who knows? What I do know is that I've never met anyone who could really understand me. Not that there's much to understand. It's just — a feeling, you know? Sometimes you see someone and you think maybe this person is just like me. [*Pause*] But it never turns out that way.
[*Pause*]
SLAYTE: I thought I met someone like that once. Less than two weeks I knew him. [*Pause*] Do you know I was with a man for three years and he was a total stranger? He lived in my house, ate at my table, slept in my bed, yet he hardly knew me. He knew only what he thought I was. He considered himself very tolerant, I think, you know. As if I were some anomaly he had to put up with. Or wanted to.
TREMBLAY: Did you tell him your feelings?
SLAYTE: No. He wouldn't have understood. And besides, it all goes back to that performance. You know. He might not have wanted to hear what I really had to say.
TREMBLAY: Yet you stayed with him.
SLAYTE: Sure I did. For no other reason than that he was there, I suppose. What's the difference anyway? All relationships are the same. Different faces, different bodies, but essentially, we all do the same things. We're born as clichés and we spend a lifetime proving it. Except maybe my parents.
TREMBLAY: Tell me about them.
SLAYTE: There. Now you're performing. Just what a psychiatrist is supposed to say. My whole life — a product of my childhood. Isn't that what your books tell you? You're just proving my point about clichés.

TREMBLAY: What would you like me to ask?
SLAYTE: Ask me why I'm here.
TREMBLAY: All right. Why are you here?
SLAYTE: Because I want to stop thinking about all this performing, all this falsehood. Because I don't believe in anything any more. Because I'd like to be proved wrong about everything. [*Pause*] But I'll tell you about my parents. There's really very little to tell. I was adopted as a baby. My natural mother committed suicide. My adoptive parents were kind and busy. Both were professionals. My father traveled a great deal and my mother was very ahead of her time — you know, not what you'd expect of a woman born into the last generation.
TREMBLAY: Do you see them?
SLAYTE: They died four years ago. A car crash. Father was on a business trip and, for once, Mother went with him. They were going to see some of the country from below. They always flew.
TREMBLAY: I'm sorry.
SLAYTE: Yes. Well, it's been long enough now. I can talk about them now that they've become a happy memory. It took me a long time to get to this point. Two, three years, I think. Do you know, right after the accident, I thought I'd go crazy, no one to talk to. I went to the university and made an appointment with a professor. Can't even remember what faculty. Some arts faculty. Then I went in there and instead of talking about courses or whatever I was supposed to talk about, I told him about the accident. [*Pause*] He was a total stranger, you see. I could tell him all my private thoughts. And he listened, I'll give him that. He may have been surprised, but he listened. I felt a lot better about it after that talk.
TREMBLAY: Were you close to your parents?
SLAYTE: As close as anyone can get to parents, I suppose. But like I said, they were busy. In and out a lot. I was very independent very early. It's better that way. You learn to rely

on your own resources. That's what Mother used to say. On yourself, so to speak. Then you never need anyone. I mean, you can *want* someone, but you never *need* that person. It's safer that way.
[*Pause*]
SLAYTE: Back to my parents. What else can I tell you? I didn't know I was adopted. And I have a box which my birth mother left for me. Filled with bits of notes, diaries. Stuff like that. I like to think we are very alike. I figured it all out. Traced it back to Barkerville. Just names and possible dates, really. It doesn't matter now anyway. It's all the past and who can do anything about that? [*Pause*] I think people spend far too much time dwelling on the past, don't you? I mean, even this conversation we're having is becoming the past as soon as it's said. So, we can't change it, can we?
TREMBLAY: Would you like to change the past?
SLAYTE: No. Yes. Well — parts of it maybe. Oh, what's the use of thinking about it?
TREMBLAY: Tell me what you'd change.
SLAYTE: Well, there was the man I mentioned that I was wrong about. I'd change that. [*Pause*] Not what I did, I mean. I'd make him be what I wanted him to be. [*Long Pause*] Do you know that I write things down a lot. Because then I can get everything said that I want to say without any interruptions. I read an article once about intimacy. And some expert or other suggested tasks two people should do to achieve that elusive state. One of these tasks was to sit together for a half-hour and for each one to talk about himself or herself without the other person interrupting. Not only that, but the person talking could only talk about him or herself. I thought that was very interesting. [*Pause*] Of course, you'd never get a man to agree to that. I get the same satisfaction out of writing things down. Only thing is, I achieve intimacy only with my paper. [*Laughs*].
TREMBLAY: Did you ever show the man you lived with what

you wrote?

SLAYTE: Good grief, no. Well, that's not entirely true. When I moved out, I left him a poem. But, you know, he had no reference for it. I wonder if he understood any of it. [*Pause*] What I started to say about writing things down, though, is — well, you'll probably think I'm crazy saying this — but . . . the thing is, I can make up something about the way I want things to be, or think they are, or whatever, and just about all the time, it happens that way. Once I've written something down, I'm almost afraid to read it because I know it's going to come true. Does this sound crazy? It's as if I'm creating things, you know? Making up my life before it happens. The chicken and the egg. Well, it can't all be coincidence if it keeps happening, can it?

TREMBLAY: The subconscious is a very powerful part of you.

SLAYTE: Oh, you think I know what I'm going to do and I simply write it down before I do it?

TREMBLAY: Is it not possible?

SLAYTE: Well, that would work if it were only me I was talking about. But the other people I write about, they do the things I say they'll do too. I mean, I'm not claiming to be some crazy prophet or anything, but, well, how do you explain it?

TREMBLAY: It could just be insightful observation.

SLAYTE: Maybe. But I think it's more than that.

TREMBLAY: Would you bring in some of the things you've written?

SLAYTE: I've given up writing. And all the stuff I had, I left in — I left it at the last place I was. Like I said, I don't want to know any more. [*Pause*] I'm not sure why I came. No. That's a lie. I need someone to talk to. I've done a terrible thing. Do you know anything about legends?

TREMBLAY: Legends? Mythology?

SLAYTE: Indian mythology. West Coast.

TREMBLAY: No, I'm sorry.

SLAYTE: It doesn't matter. I don't even know why I asked. [*Pause*] Thank you for seeing me. May I come back?
TREMBLAY: Certainly. Next week?
SLAYTE: Fine.
TREMBLAY: Were you referred by your family doctor?
SLAYTE: No. I'd prefer to keep this between you and me.
TREMBLAY: With a referral, you would be covered under your medical plan.
SLAYTE: No. I'll take care of it, if it's all the same.
TREMBLAY: As you wish. Monday next?
SLAYTE: That would be fine.
TREMBLAY: My secretary will give you the time. Thank you for coming and I'll look forward to our next meeting.

TAPE #2: MAY 4, 1987.

SLAYTE: Today, I would like to play a game. I will tell you things and you have to decide what's true and what isn't.
DR. TREMBLAY: All right.
SLAYTE: I am a daughter with no parents. I am a voice with no sound. I am a myth with no creator. I am a song with no music. I am a mother with no child.
TREMBLAY: [*Pause*] You're speaking in riddles.
SLAYTE: But that's what you're here for, isn't it? You're supposed to figure me out.
TREMBLAY: I'm here to help you understand yourself. Suppose you explain your riddles.
SLAYTE: [*Sigh*] Simple. Simple. A daughter with no parents. True. A voice with no sound. True.
TREMBLAY: True how?
SLAYTE: We already talked about this last time. My true voice is written, so it has no sound.

TREMBLAY: Go on.
SLAYTE: A myth with no creator. True. And don't ask how. You don't know anything about legends. A song without music. False.
TREMBLAY: Explain.
SLAYTE: What's there to explain? How can there be a song without music? It would be a verse, or a poem. There's no such thing as a song without music. It's false. I don't want to play this game any more.
TREMBLAY: What about the last one?
SLAYTE: I said I don't want to play any more.
TREMBLAY: All right. What would you like to talk about?
SLAYTE: Nothing. I don't have anything to say today, so you can just shut off that silly tape recorder. It's making me nervous. [*Pause*] Just who will you be playing that for?
TREMBLAY: No one. It's confidential. What goes on between us remains confidential.
SLAYTE: Well, I don't see why you have to bother to record it, then. If it's only for the two of us. We both know what we're saying. [*Pause*] Do you know what happens to people when they get very old? They forget the past. And they forget what a future is. They become totally concerned with the present. With every minute detail as it happens, no matter how inconsequential it is. Sarah was like this.
TREMBLAY: Sarah?
SLAYTE: Yes. But you don't know who Sarah is. It doesn't matter. She has become part of the past. Another memory. I learned a lot from Sarah. [*Pause*] But — I remember now things she said or did much better than when they happened. They were not a memory then. Do you think I have made Sarah up?
TREMBLAY: Not if you say she existed.
SLAYTE: Well, I have made her up. I have made Sarah into a myth. She was only an old woman. But I have forgotten that. I'm good at making up myths. [*Pause*] And there's David.

TREMBLAY: David?
SLAYTE: David. Another myth of mine. He is the man I told you about. The one I met once and would have changed. [*Pause*] Perhaps he never existed. No. That's a lie. I have proof. I had proof.
[*Pause*]
TREMBLAY: Go on.
SLAYTE: There's nothing more to go on with. [*Pause*] You know, I think we make everything up, don't we? Like the way we perform. We recount our past, but not really the way it happened. We change it. That's what we do. We tell tragedies as comedies and comedies as tragedies. Even the inane can become significant in the retelling. [*Pause*] It's like fiction. A synthesized version of the truth, which, if reported realistically, would be boring. Take right now, for instance. This is not a memory to recall. However, years from now, I will tell someone about this meeting, this moment. And I will say things like, "She had an old tape recorder which made a whining sound at irregular intervals. And sometimes, it was as if Dr. Tremblay orchestrated the sound to coincide with something I said. It was like being gonged." Silly, isn't it? And totally untrue? But it would make this moment much more memorable, don't you agree?
TREMBLAY: If you say so.
SLAYTE: If you say so. If you say so. Why don't you tell me what *you* think.
TREMBLAY: I'm not here to discuss what I think.
SLAYTE: No, you wouldn't be. Well, I'm tired of telling you what I think. I don't want to think any more. I'm sick of it.
[*Pause*]
TREMBLAY: All right. I'll see you again next week? Same time?
SLAYTE: I don't know what good it'll do. I don't feel any different.
TREMBLAY: These things take time.

SLAYTE: I don't have much time. I may be going away.
TREMBLAY: But you'll be back?
SLAYTE: I don't know. [*Pause*] I probably won't be going before next week, though.
TREMBLAY: Monday then?
SLAYTE: Sure. Monday. For all the good it'll do.

TAPE #3: MAY 11, 1987.

SLAYTE: Do you believe in cycles?
DR. TREMBLAY: It depends.
SLAYTE: What kind of answer is that? Either you do or you don't. [*Pause*] Well, I suppose you don't then, or you wouldn't have to qualify it.
TREMBLAY: Ummm.
SLAYTE: I think sometimes that everything is predestined. You know. We can't help the things we do.
TREMBLAY: But last week, you said you think you make things happen.
SLAYTE: True. But maybe what I'm making up was there to begin with. Like memories. [*Pause*] Do you want to hear about David?
TREMBLAY: If you want to talk about him.
SLAYTE: I saw him again. A few months later. But I didn't recognize him. Oh, not physically. I mean we were together again but we were not together. Do you understand?
TREMBLAY: I think so.
SLAYTE: He was better as a myth. [*Pause*] I've had his baby, you know. It was the completion of a cycle. Now everything is back to normal. Fulfilled. I may be going away. Did I tell you?
TREMBLAY: Tell me about the baby.
SLAYTE: No. I have no baby.

TREMBLAY: But you just said . . .
SLAYTE: Never mind what I said. You mustn't believe everything I say. I may be going away. Do you believe me?
TREMBLAY: Where are you going?
SLAYTE: I am going to live on an island. "Man is an island." It's not technically true, you know. Not unless you're surrounded by water. Do you think we are responsible for everything we do?
TREMBLAY: Do you?
SLAYTE: No. I mean, some things just happen. Or are meant to happen. Like death. Well, you can't be responsible for death, can you? It's a universal terminal disease. [*Laugh*].
TREMBLAY: What about death?
SLAYTE: What about it? Without death there would be no life. The opposite ends of a spectrum. Do you gamble?
TREMBLAY: Gamble?
SLAYTE: Yes. Yes. Gamble. You know. Cards, crap tables, lotteries, whatever. Do you?
TREMBLAY: No.
SLAYTE: You lie. Being alive is a gamble. It wouldn't be worth living without the death odds. I mean, imagine immortality. There'd be no point to anything really. Without the gamble, immortality would mean you could do everything eventually, and because of that, you'd do nothing. Or everything. It would have no meaning either way. I'm tired of living. Do you believe me?
TREMBLAY: You're very young. You've hardly begun to live.
SLAYTE: Oh, what do you know about living? You and your middle-class existence, your boring, predictable, existence? It's like immortality. Knowing your life will forever more be the same as it is now. I couldn't bear it. You're already dead only you don't know it.
TREMBLAY: But you can never really predict what will happen. There is no certainty as you describe it. And what about people?

You can't anticipate the human element.

SLAYTE: You're wrong. People can only make a difference if you let them near you. And I don't believe in that, remember? I have abandoned my baby. No intimacy. No responsibility. Do you believe me? [*Pause*] Well, don't answer then. It doesn't matter anyway. Maybe I made that up too. What I told you about my parents? It's not true. Do you want to hear the real story?

TREMBLAY: If you want to tell it to me.

SLAYTE: So predictable. What a cliché you are. We all are. Well, I'll tell you the story. You see, I was adopted by chance. My parents found me in the bottom of a canoe which had been floating at sea for days, weeks maybe. They thought I was a good omen. Do you believe me?

TREMBLAY: No.

SLAYTE: Well . . . it's true of the mythical me. Anyway, what's important is that they found me. Or I them. Do you believe in the Underworld?

TREMBLAY: Do you mean Hell?

SLAYTE: No, not Hell. You can only believe in Hell if you believe in Heaven. There is no God. I mean the Underworld. A world under the sea, under the earth, under your skin. A world from which you can't escape. Nor want to. [*Pause*] But you, you would never find the passageway. No. Because you don't believe in loons whose eyes can make tunnels in a black sea, nor in flatfish who carry the burdens of eternity on their bellies. I have ridden both. Do you believe me?

TREMBLAY: Yes, metaphorically.

SLAYTE: Oh you are a bore. I'm going away. Did I tell you?

TREMBLAY: Yes.

SLAYTE: I won't be seeing you any more. Do you believe me?

TREMBLAY: Where are you going?

SLAYTE: I'm going to the Middleworld. Do you know what that is?

TREMBLAY: No.

SLAYTE: It's a place between this one and the Underworld. A place where misfits fit. Do you believe me?

TREMBLAY: Yes.

SLAYTE: No, you don't. You're only saying that. Performing again. Do you want to know why I'm going to the Middleworld? I'm going there to build mountains and rivers. I'm going there to meet my mother, my daughter. I'm going there to guard the land against the intrusion of men. Do you believe me? Do you believe me?

TREMBLAY: Yes.

[Pause]

SLAYTE: No. You don't understand anything. That's why you don't believe. I won't be coming back. Do you believe that?

TREMBLAY: Elise, I'd like you to keep coming to see me for a while longer.

SLAYTE: I can't. There's nothing more to tell. You can't help me. No one can.

TREMBLAY: I'd like to try. Will you come next week?

SLAYTE: And if I say no? What will you do? You can't keep me here. [Pause] I'll come again. If I'm still here.

"She never came back," Dr. Tremblay says to Paul. "I hadn't really expected her to."

She sits behind her desk, hands on her lap, Paul thinks, because he can't see them. He wonders if she is taping their conversation.

"You have no address for her?" he asks. "Didn't she say anything else? Before or after you switched on the tape?"

"Nothing. She paid in cash. Not even a medical number. She said she was just traveling through."

Paul sighs. "I thought you might like to know that the baby's been placed."

Dr. Tremblay leans forward and puts both elbows on the

table. "What about my client?"

"She hasn't been found. It's a big country. She could be anywhere."

"There's nothing more you can do?"

"We'll keep the file open. The baby's fine. That's what matters now. She may turn up."

After thanking Dr. Tremblay, Paul returns to his office. He takes the file out and re-reads parts of it.

She has disappeared. It is as if she never existed. Paul slaps the file closed. Annie calls him on another matter. He has lunch. In the evening, he watches a movie, then the news. He has a glass of scotch — neat — and goes to bed. He resumes the repetitive cycles of his existence.

On weekends, when weather permits, Paul rents a boat and goes to Porcher Island. He never moors anywhere, simply skirts the banks, facing the ocean

because it is believed that anyone who sets eyes on the woman of the island becomes trapped forever in that middle world.

CODA

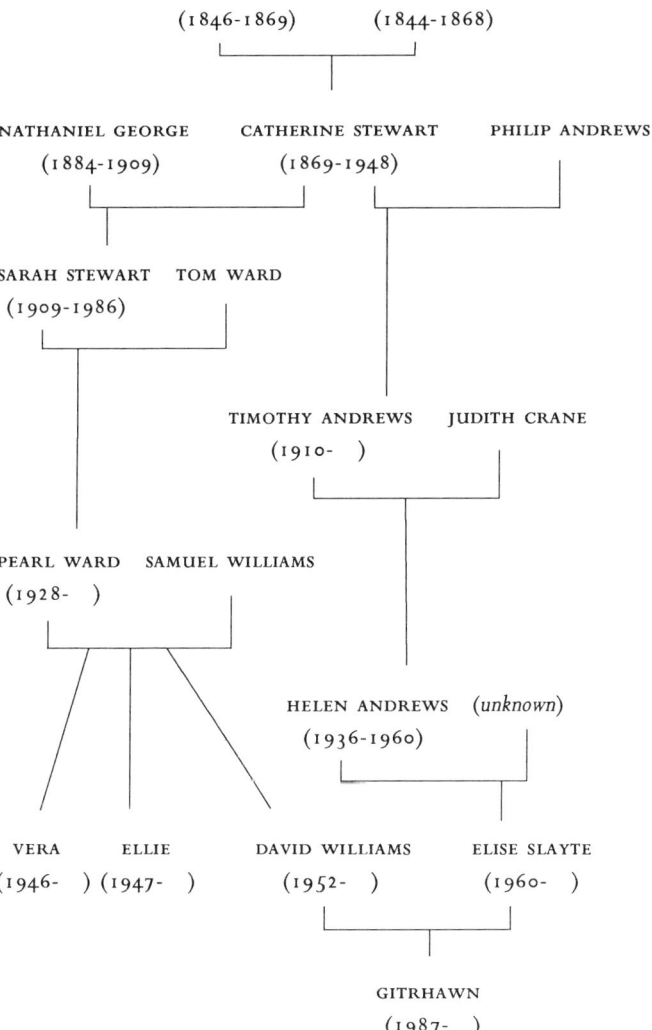